For the Life of Me

her story

by Jeanette Stone Bishop

NUOVA EDITORIA
2014

AUTHOR'S NOTE

Everything in these stories is true to the best of my memory. Clearly I have imagined the details of some things, because they just don't add up the way I have always thought of them. However the gist of everything is true. Except a couple of names which I substituted for the real person, either because I can't remember the name or because I believe they might prefer not to have their names in a book, and I have no way to check with them about that. And except for a little fun mention of some lint which may or may not have existed. And maybe something about a leprechaun.

For...
Christy, Rick, Littlejohn, Leila, Scott, Todd, Casey, and Jennifer

Thanks to...

Bob Welch, founder of Beachside Writers, and cohort Jane Kirkpatrick for their unfailing inspiration, superior teaching, and encouragement. Roger Hite for his unmatched generosity in teaching, technical assistance, time, and support.

Scott Bishop for untold hours of reading, editing, technical assistance in the process, and for his support and patience, John Bishop for designing my cover, working on and arranging pictures, Todd Bishop for supplying pictures and scanning old negatives, Christy Bishop Cricow for digging out and scanning pictures, reading and editing, and for all of their artistic counsel and encouragement in the midst of their overly busy lives.

My brother Boyd Stone and cousin Bette Hockema for helping me remember to the best of their ability, Ruth Lefevre for agreeing to scan the book at the last minute for glitches, and for sound advice, Ann Sessions for suggesting that I should start writing, and my Creative Writing group at Campbell Center for keeping me going for the last three years with their support, encouragement, superb writing, polite listening to my apologies, and still remaining friendly.

CONTENTS

WHAT WILL THEY FIND?

When I am gone
After my time has passed
Will they be surprised at anything

Will they know the songs I used to sing
Will they ever know I once was young
As limber as that new tree
Will they know that I once had some skill
Or could have had
Given the time—the choice—the will

Will they recognize the butter pat
That wooden homemade paddle
Or will it be lightly tossed aside
Not known it was carved by my father with pride
Will they know that cup was his
That old cup of tin
Or lightly—it's nothing, no value
Right in the recyle bin
Will they know who gave me the pearls
Will it matter to them
Nobody wears them anymore
Especially not young girls

Will they wish they had asked
Before time had passed
There must be a thousand things
I value beyond measure

To be found in boxes chests and drawers
Just to be gotten rid of quick
A lifetime of lore and treasure

Gone with the wind

I had a neighbor across the way
She was an old lady to me
Friendly tall Ingrid who walked every day
Slowly—carefully—stepping—just so
She cried
When I told her my mother had died
I made her baked goods sometimes
She gave me fruit from her vines
We spoke of figs and quinces—changing times

There must have been much for her to tell
Maybe I didn't listen so well
In her gazebo a time or two
We sat and had some tea
Enjoyed her nasturtiums roses and mums
While time continued to flee

At the estate sale I learned so much more
There were things I had never dreamed
Things that touched me to the core
White linens and pieces of lace
She'd lovingly ironed and put in their place
For somebody else to find

Delicate china, demitasse, glass
Books to enrich the mind
Teacups, candlesticks, silver, plates
Having folks in for tea
I had to imagine her rich young past
She'd been an old lady to me

It was only after 35 years had gone by
That I learned when the end was nigh
That Ingrid, my old friend had once been
The Sweetheart of Sigma Chi

A LETTER TO MY FORMER SELF

Hello, girl! Turning 16, huh? Big day for you.

This is your alter ego speaking. I know more about you, not everything, but more than anybody else ever has or ever will. I know you like the idea of being sixteen, but I don't even know how you are spending your day.

I do know that Daddy died two years ago, and you are still feeling great loss and grief. That will always be with you. There is nothing good about it, but it will make you appreciate some things more than you otherwise would.

I want to talk with you about some things that only you and I know.

You have some regrets already. Well, you will have more of those, knowing you.

There was a time during Daddy's long illness that your friends were all going skating, and he asked you to stay home that night. He needed you there. You were torn, but you were weak, and you went. You needed to go and have some release and normal fun. His days had to have been long and almost unendurable for all those 24 months. Maybe he understood, as nothing more was said about it. You were lucky nobody was mad at you. And of course most nights you were there. Maybe Mom intervened and helped him understand. She also had to have been so tired and discouraged, taking care of him that way for those two years. But she often showed surprising wisdom. You thought she was old. But she was only 48 when he died.

11

Sometime you will know how young that was.

You didn't do all bad.

After a year or so of Daddy's illness, you thought of a solution. Every night you prayed for hours, or what seemed like hours, as long as you could fight off sleep, asking that he be made well again. You knew that was the answer. This went on for many months. You never gave up. Even though no one was listening.

Another good thing you did one day was when you sat on the side of Daddy's bed and took his hand. Daddy had beautiful hands. They still looked young and strong though he was increasingly thin. Nothing was said. You just held his hand for a long time.

Eventually Daddy said, "Why are you holding my hand? Is it because you think I want you to?" You said, "Yeah". You thought, "I should let go". But you felt such overwhelming love for him and just continued to hang on. It filled your throat. Your answer to him wasn't true; you weren't doing it for him; you were doing it for yourself. He may have known how you were feeling. For one of the few times in your life, you were living in the moment, and you will never forget it. You will always be glad you did that, and you'll be able to recapture that feeling of deepest closeness though your time with him was so short.

There are other good memories. Like the hot summer day you went with Daddy to Myrtle Point when you were 10 or 11 and stopped at Norway on the way back for a big ice cream bar, vanilla covered with milk chocolate and nuts. Norway consists of one store, which sits on a grassy knoll halfway between Coquille and Myrtle Point. A big sign on the front says, "Stop and See the Mayor." You ate those ice cream bars, and they were gone by the time you were almost home.

Daddy said, "That was so good, I want another one, don't you?" You'd never known you could eat two ice cream bars in a row. But you said, "Sure", happily. You also had never known that one of your parents would drive that far for such foolishness. He turned around and drove back the three or four miles and bought two more. I don't think you ever told Mom about that little wayward indulgence. But if you had she would have just laughed.

Norway store will be gone in a few years. But that memory never will.

You will also remember going to a baseball game with Daddy, and will hold a fondness for baseball ever after.

You will remember Daddy's infectious laugh and the funny stories he told on himself. He sort of wheezed instead of hah-hahahing when he laughed. His sister, Aunt Nannie laughed that way too, and frankly, so do you.

You'll remember the many times that you listened to Daddy and Uncle Cince talking politics, expounding on, and agreeing about everything, both being good Democrats. You asked Daddy a question sometimes after those sessions, and learned a little, such as what a tariff is.

And listening to Daddy and Dr. Richmond. He would be called out when Daddy was having a particularly bad time, would get him feeling better, and they would start talking politics. Every time they would get into a big argument, ending when Dr. Richmond had the last word and went stomping out, both of them mad as hornets. You will always remember that and laugh. Those times were educational for you and will stay with you forever, as it turned you into a political junky. You didn't always agree with Daddy. You knew sometimes Dr. Richmond was right. But you rightfully forgave Daddy and understood that he hadn't had all the opportunities that the doctor had and that you will have.

You started high school a couple of years ago. The third day was summery and warm. You got off the bus after school, sweaty, and tired, and walked down the gravel driveway at home, where some uncles and neighborhood men stood talking quietly, some of them having a smoke. Nobody seemed to notice that you were there. So you stood holding an armload of heavy books. Afraid to ask. Afraid to go inside. You felt invisible and just stood there—forever—in the hot sun.

Finally Mom stepped outside and saw you.

Daddy had gone into a coma. The women were inside. You went in then.

You were standing at the foot of Daddy's bed, alone in the room, gazing at him. Suddenly, for no reason that you could discern, you felt an uncontrollable urge to laugh. You couldn't stop. You were afraid somebody would come in and see you, so you went into the kitchen, empty of people, and stayed in the corner until you got yourself under control. That confused you. It was something like telephone wires getting crossed and sending mixed messages.

You will grow up, and the pain will change from acute to chronic.

And some of the painful shyness will pass. You will find out it usually isn't worth the energy it takes to be shy. What if you do say the wrong thing sometimes? It probably won't hurt anybody but yourself, and then only if you let it. Anyway people aren't as concerned with you as you think.

Some things I am not going to tell you about your future. I am going to let you enjoy the dreams of happy times, of getting married and living together until old age with an intact happy family.

You might as well believe that you will grow up and become a great teacher, an actress, a comedienne, a musician, or a detective. Those are some of the things you want to be.

Some of your dreams might come true. You will feel lucky for other things in your life—for a wonderful happy marriage as long as it lasts. And wonderful children. You don't have to know everything that is going to happen. You will deal with it as it occurs.

Don't let anybody tell you that bad things are good things. They will try, but they don't know. They think they will make you feel better by telling you that huge losses are okay because they were ordained by some greater power. If that comforts them, let them be comforted, without your rancor. Just let it go.

You will be stronger. You will suffer alone. You will share some of the good things. Some you will enjoy alone.

Enjoy what is good to the fullest. Live in the moment more often. And know when you've been lucky.

Work for the important things. Know that you will never be good enough. You will fail your children and others at times. But do your best as often as you can. The rest of the time, try to figure out why you can't, and forgive yourself now and then. Forgive others too. They are all doing the best they can.

Except maybe for some politicians.

By the way, girl—I'm 80 now! Just think how lucky that is! I used to be your age.

OUR COUNTRY HOUSE

1

It seems like a good idea to start the story of my life by describing the house where I first lived and grew up—the big porch surrounding the front and one side, the porch swing squeaking like a young bird's chirp as we sat sipping lemonade, the wisteria climbing over the arbor, my room upstairs, and rowdy kids running all over.

The great expanse of green lawns surrounded by lush shrubbery where the siblings ran barefoot like wild animals at play, and where my dignified uncles and aunts came by on weekends to play croquet, followed by brisk and stimulating conversation, enriching my life. I was rarely alone. At the fair, there was always somebody to ride with on the merry-go-round as we all scrambled to get on the horse we wanted.

But that would be fiction. Here's the way it really was.

While five of my mother's most respectable siblings with their families, and my maternal grandparents, lived within a half-mile of us, the word dignified didn't apply. And I doubt if any of them ever played croquet.

Before I was born in 1931, my dad decided to go into business. So he had a Union 76 Service Station built on the property with a pair of tourist cabins a few yards behind it.

It was during the depression, and Daddy couldn't make a go of it. He gave away most of the gas because few could afford to pay for it, and he couldn't turn away anybody in need. "Well, what are they going to do?" he would say. There were no tourists to rent the cabins. So he kept his saw-filing job at the logging camp.

Rereading Daddy's business log years later, we saw where he'd written, "Paid with tears," by some of the entries.

Mama had to drop everything and run out to pump gas for people who came by during those days. She'd say, "Oh, there's somebody else out there wanting gas. I wish we'd never gotten that station,"

My brother was born in an old one-bedroom camp house, which my father had bought for $100 and moved onto the place. They moved from it into the two newer, nicer cabins shortly before my appearance on the scene, and sold the old house for $10 to old man Kaufman, who moved it to nearby Glen Aiken Creek where he lived in it for years, but never could come up with the $10.

The cabins they moved into were each about 10 by 15 feet, the size of one medium bedroom, divided by a partial wall. A third of the space served as a kitchen with a low counter and sink along the back wall, and a wood stove for cooking and heat. The larger space could hold a double bed and a little drop-leaf table and chairs under the window.

The two cabins added up to 300 square feet for a family of four once I'd entered the picture. They removed the counter and stove from one unit to turn it into a bedroom for the whole family, freeing the other to accommodate the round oak table and chairs, the old wooden rocker, the radio, and a narrow Hoosier-style cabinet with bins for flour and sugar. It might be called a "great room" of the period. A kitchen, dining room, and living room all in one. That eliminated the heat source and running water from the bedroom end of the house. The bathroom facility was outside.

The two cabins, connected by an unfinished double garage with a gravel floor and no doors, made the whole structure 40 feet long and required us to go outside to get to the bedroom each night, often having to make a run for it through the Oregon mist or frequent downpours. I remember a lot of squealing and giggling on that evening ritual, as I bounced in the arms of whoever made the jog with me. I was carried for a good part of the four years that we lived in those circumstances.

Well, it was a house, sort of. And it was in the country.

The well-built cabins were cute with pretty flower garden linoleum, but icy cold to step onto with bare feet in the mornings as we crawled out from under heavy quilts.

Periodically Mama and Daddy, tore into the rooms with new paint and changed the colors. The walls and ceilings, finished with three-inch bead board, became soft yellow, white, blue, or pink. Each unit had two small-paned casement windows which opened in, plus a windowed door to outside. Mama hung crisp organdy curtains that she bought at Penny's and replaced when they got shabby from many washings. Sometimes they were white with red trim, others white with blue dots, or yellow, or green. Each unit had two bare light bulbs, one in the middle of each ceiling.

19

You turned them on by pulling a twine string attached to the chain hanging from the white porcelain fixture.

For a little added luxury in the bedroom, Daddy lengthened the string to reach up the length of the double bed and tied it to the iron-tubed head so all they did was reach up and pull, to turn the light on or off without getting up. Headboards also served as a handy place to stick your gum in case you were chewing some Juicy Fruit or Beeman's when you went to bed. You wouldn't want to lose it and find it in your hair. Anyway you might want another chew in the morning. It didn't occur to me to wonder how that fitted in to our dental hygiene. We brushed our teeth every night but must have followed up with putting the gum back in our mouths afterward. No, we weren't unique in that bad habit. There was even a popular song about it. "Does the chewing gum lose its flavor on the bed post overnight?"

I've wondered how we kept our clothes in those first years. No closet of any kind existed in either cabin. The dresser had drawers. Mama folded my clothes and laid them in a varnished fir chest that Daddy had made, with my starched cotton dresses lying on top just under the lid. But we each had a coat, Daddy had a suit, and Mama, several dresses. They must have driven some nails for those. My brother, 90 now, is the only one left I have to ask about these things, and he can't remember any more than I do.

But we had a porch. At the kitchen door. One step up from the dirt and gravel, it held everything that wouldn't fit inside. Mama loved her gray square Maytag wringer washer and double wash tubs for rinsing. She often said, "I just love to wash."

Every Monday I watched her put on her apron after getting dressed, fixing breakfast, cleaning up, and starting the big pot of beans cooking. Then she sorted the clothes into piles of whites, coloreds and darks. I helped a little, watched her load them into the sudsy, steaming tub, and listened to the hollow whump-whump, whump-whump as the machine threw the dirty clothes from side to side for 20 minutes before she ran each load through the wringer and into the rinse water, through the wringer again into the bluing, and through the wringer again into the basket.

We could also hear the soft sounds of the Burbanks' washing machine just down the hill from our house, wafting out and around on Monday mornings, greeting the new week.

Out to the clothes line where I handed her the clothes pins, watched, and listened as she snapped the wet dish towels before pinning them up. In the afternoon, we inhaled the good smells of the sun-dried clothes as we brought them in, folded, and sprinkled for ironing on Tuesday. Just like in the nursery rhyme, "Monday, Washing, Tuesday, Ironing—"

Above the tubs, wooden shelves held bars of Fels Naptha soap, a bottle of Mrs. Stewart's bluing, a jug of Purex, clothes pins, and sprinkling bottle. The ironing board, a rag mop, the kind with a clamp to hold a real rag that you could take out and wash or replace when it wore completely out, and the broom, leaned against the wall. The mop bucket, McNess iron dust pan, which I still have and use 80 years later, and a copper boiler in which Mama had to heat water on the stove and make several trips with to fill the washer and rinse tubs every Monday, fitted in somewhere. Then there was the big galvanized tub that came into the kitchen every Saturday night when we all had baths whether we needed them or not.

Our house must have looked like the grapes of wrath from the outside.

The welcome mat was a burlap bag that cow feed had come in, folded outside the door for foot wiping. Another one served as a bed for my Pekingese, Toby. On the exterior wall by the back door hung the cooler, screened to let air in and keep bugs out. That's where enameled pans of milk sat to let the cream rise to the top for pouring on cereals, whipping, and making butter. Fortunately, we went through the skimmed milk pretty fast and you let the cream sour to make the best butter. We kept other food there to stay as cool as weather permitted.

When the cream was ready, Boyd and I sat in the middle of the floor and took turns churning. Daddy or Mama, collected up the butter with the butter pat, placed the big glob on a plate, and drank the buttermilk that was left. Or if she had some corn bread, Mama broke it up into a glass, poured the buttermilk over it, and ate it with a spoon. "If I could have only one thing to eat, it would be corn bread and buttermilk," she said. I was happy for her to have all the buttermilk she wanted.

Across from the kitchen sink hung an eight by ten mirror and Daddy's razor strop. All the washing up, teeth brushing, washing hair, and shaving had to be done there as it was the only running water in the house, and cold at that.

I frequently watched Daddy in an undershirt with his suspenders hanging down in loops at his sides, work up a lather, brush it over his face, and shave. A graceful operation with a straight razor as his hands maneuvered it over his face and under the chin. Then he combed his jet black hair, put on his blue work shirt, and snapped the suspenders into place before taking off for work.

During springs and summers, almost always a bouquet of bright daffodils, poppies, or dahlias from Mama's flower gardens, brightened the room, centered on a crocheted doily on the round oak table. As I got big enough, I sometimes picked the bouquets.

It was a happy place with lots of laughter. In later years, Mom told about how we used to all go to bed, somebody would get up and go get in with Mama and Daddy, one of them would get crowded out, then another one would come get in, and the other would change beds. And we all got up in the morning, out of a different bed than we'd started in the night before.

It wasn't dire poverty. We ate well, and we were happy and well-cared-for. The only problem for me was that I felt bored and alone much of the time. "What is there to do?" Mama would suggest something. "Why don't you go down and see Mrs. Osborne. Pick her some flowers," or "Go make a daisy chain," or "Get your color book and color."

Trips on the weekends took us to the beach, the Liberty Theater to see a show occasionally, or visiting. I just imagined more and wider horizons.

When our family got up in the mornings, we never sat down again except to eat. After supper Daddy and Boyd turned on the radio sometimes, and sat to listen. But Mama cleaned up and worked 'til bedtime. I stood around mostly, and maybe wiped some dishes if Mama insisted.

The only time I know of Mama sitting down during the day was when she got a copy of *Gone with the Wind*, and couldn't put it down until some days later when she finished it. She was always ashamed of herself for that dalliance. But she laughed about it. Other than that, the first time I knew you could sit down during the day, except for school and church where you had to, was after I was grown and around my in-laws. They were "city people" and knew about that. And I picked up on it pretty fast even though it felt a little odd at first.

When I was still four, we loaded up the Model A Ford with everything we could fit into it, and moved to a logging camp up Coos River at Allegany, a small community where we took a ferry across the river on the way up. We made that temporary move for Daddy's job. I had my fifth birthday up there, and after about a year we moved back home.

While we were gone some distant relatives of Mama's, who had just moved to Oregon from Arkansas, lived in the house. They just about demolished the place. Or they might have, given more time there. When they ran out of firewood, they chopped up three of the four oak dining chairs. And turned them to ash. The dining set was the one new thing Mama and Daddy had bought for themselves, for $20, when they were first married in 1921. The "renters" (I doubt that they paid any rent; we probably just let them live there) threw all their garbage out the kitchen window, so

24

we had a pile of tin cans, boxes and rotting food scraps to clean up. And when a door didn't close quite properly, they fixed it with an ax.

"Oh, no, the chairs are gone," and "What happened to the door?" and "Oh, my goodness, look out here. What will we do with all this mess?" But my parents took everything in stride. They just handled whatever came along. Nobody got overly excited or upset about anything.

So just in time apparently, we took the house over again. Daddy started working on it and turned the garage into a living room. For the first time, you could walk from the kitchen to the bedroom without going outside. He took great pride in the new fir floor that he sanded by hand on his knees, and varnished to a fine sheen. They covered the living room walls with embossed rose-colored wall paper, and bought a wine wool rug, three patterned scatter rugs, and a pair of chairs with wooden arms and padded seats and backs, from Purkey's Furniture in Coquille. That's the first upholstery we ever owned. To me it felt like the ultimate in glamour. I could hardly wait to walk on the newly varnished floor, and when I did, I felt like a princess.

A wood stove went in the living room, and became our central heating.

When I was eight, my parents went to a house in town where the people were selling most of their belongings, and paid $50 for a light-oak piano that changed my life. They generously threw in for me a life size "walking doll" with long curls. I'd never seen one before and couldn't believe it was mine. I was entranced.

Around then we also bought a cute little couch, our

first, with red plaid fabric, from a neighbor. I think it cost us $8. It didn't match our decor, but it was another seat so several people could all sit down at once. And it was another piece of upholstery. All in all things were looking up.

Most people wouldn't consider our house adequate, even with a living room. But sounds of a crackling fire in the cook stove, the smell of fried chicken, a big pot of beans, or baking bread, and the whole family sitting on straight chairs or on the floor—well, except Mama—listening to "One Man's Family" or "Lum and Abner" on the new Sentinel radio, filled it with warmth and love.

Even before the living room, it was far better than the romantic fantasy of a two-story house with the big front porch and the passel of rowdy kids that I sometimes pictured. It set the stage for my life in ways that I didn't know at the time, like an upside down pyramid.

I dreamed a lot, but never imagined the events and places I would experience, the houses I would live in, and the people I would know and love.

I just knew there was a bigger world out there somewhere.

[Family]

[Father's Gas Station]

THE ROCKS

2

The perfectly round river rocks were big enough to sit on, and, as a child, I made good use of them. They lined the front edge of our yard, giving it a little structure to divide us from the road and were a landmark for people driving Highway 42, to know when they'd arrived at Johnson Hill. In case anybody would want to know that. Or maybe Daddy had them there to signify that this is where the Stones live.

They'd always been there to my knowledge. At some point Daddy, obviously with help since you couldn't budge one of them from its spot, brought them from a river where, over the ages, they had been washed into works of art— great orbs, about 18 inches in diameter. I suppose they were sandstone with their grainy texture and gray color of beach sand, the only ones I've ever seen. But I always thought that they were river rocks. Much later my brother told me they'd come from Sunset Bay on the Pacific coast, about 25 or 30 miles from us.

There were eight or ten of them, most evenly spaced in

a curved row across the front, but one was by the goldfish pond and one or two others here and there.

Behind the rocks was what we called "the lawn". It had some grass, but mostly weeds, the most memorable of which were the "snake heads", little oval shaped knobs on top of stiff stems that bobbed and made hollow clunking noises as your oxfords hit them when you walked through, sounding like tom toms on a drum set. And the little white daisies that many people who have real lawns try to kill, but that Mama taught me to make daisy chains out of early on. In fact those daisies were Aunt Verna's favorite flower, and she even sowed them in her lawn. We always associated them with her.

We had three acres which included a big field with vegetable gardens, a barn and fenced field for the cow, a pen for the pig, and a chicken house with a yard for them. Daddy had a dozen healthy rhubarb plants along the fence, lots of loganberries, and plenty of cow and chicken manure to keep them lush and healthy.

That should explain the casualness of the yard. There was a lot to do. My parents and big brother worked hard. I was the littlest and never got to the point where much was expected of me except to not get in the way too much.

There was a grove of trees behind the house. I walked down there once a year in early spring, into the dense shade, near the seasonal creek, and hunted until I found the trilliums—those white, star-shaped jewels that were such a treasure. I never touched them, hiding in the shade. I left them there. For the fairies I guess, or just to keep the magic in the woods and in my mind.

Mama loved flowers. We had lots of them. I'm sure she showed me the trilliums the first time. After that I always went alone.

She had a huge dahlia bed, peonies, columbines, hydrangeas, lilacs, a snowball, sweet peas, wild sorrel, lily of the valley, daffodils, tulips, primroses, and pansies, her favorite since childhood because of their faces. Lots of yellow California poppies did their own thing. Lily pads floated on the fish pond, and the romantic little pink and white Cecile Brunner rose, famous for making the first corsage for young girls, bloomed almost the year round under the kitchen window. They came and went as flowers do.

But the rocks were always there, a good place to sit and dream. That's what I did a lot of. We were country people and proud of it. It was all I knew, but, increasingly, I tried to imagine how city life would be. I was drawn to the luxury of having sidewalks or even a "path". We called anyplace you would walk a "trail". A path through the woods or around the house sounded more elegant even if it was just dirt. But a sidewalk. You could play hopscotch or roller skate.

I don't know whether moving pictures came first or some of the poetry that was read to me, in spurring my imagination about another world, but a line from Robert Louis Stevenson's *A Child's Garden of Verses* poem, "Bed in Summer", stuck with me:

"Or hear the grown-up people's feet,
Still going past me in in the street…"

The picture of hearing people walking by under the window when I was in bed, set me to imagining what it would be like to have sidewalks.

On a Friday or Saturday night, Daddy might say, "Shall we go to the show?" "Yes!" So we all got ready and went to the Liberty. What I mostly remember of that was Shirley Temple.

So I sat on a rock and pretended to be a dancer with bouncing curls and dimpled cheeks. As time went on, I began to think that what I saw in shows, was how the real world was—always on stage, tap dancing.

So I sat on a rock, a fat, funny-looking little girl, waving at cars going by, thinking maybe somebody from far away, would come by and discover the real me, full of eagerness, ambition, and longing, and be so taken with my appearance that I would somehow be thrust out into a life of glamour, adventure, and success.

Some of the people waved back.

MOM AND GRANDMA
THE WAY THEY WERE

3

"Fiddlesticks," said Mom, "I just let my spoon slide right down into this big kettle of jam!"

"Well, that's no worse than what I'm into," said Grandma, "This plague-taked yarn just got so tangled up, I cain't get it unraveled for nothin'."

"I'm afraid this jam'll over-cook before I get that spoon out and get it off the stove."

"Well, if I don't get started on them socks, I'm never going to be ready for Christmas."

"Maybe you could make them some date candy instead of socks this year."

"No, I did that last year and had the blamedest time you ever saw. It sugared and wouldn't get hard. You can just put me away in the porehouse if I ever do that again."

"For the life of me, I don't know how I'm going to get this spoon out of here."

"Well, maybe you need to use some tongs."

"I'd use some if I had any, but I don't have any tongs."

"You, don't? Well, what ever happened to them tongs I used to have?"

"Well, mother, I don't know. It's been nine years since

you moved up here with me, and we couldn't bring all your things. I don't remember ever seeing them."

"Well I don't know why in the world we wouldn't have brought them tongs along. They would a come in real handy."

"Well, maybe we would have if we'd known I was going to lose a spoon in the jam nine years later, and if the boys had known I didn't have any when they moved you up here."

"Well, I reckon. I s'pose they didn't think about that, and I must not have either, or I'd a made sure they got 'em in."

"Yes, I imagine you would have."

"Well, at least you got the jam off the stove, so it don't cook to death."

"Yes, it'll probably be all right, but I think it's going to work me to death trying to get that spoon out without burning my hands."

"Nine years. Has it been that long? Law, I don't know where the time goes. It shore don't seem that long since I've been up here. It seems like just yesterday that I lost Ed. Well, I guess I'll be seein' him again directly. Oh, law."

"I know, the time just flies. We must be having an awful good time, the way it goes by."

"Well, I guess we are, the fix we're both in."

"Are you going to feel like going to church tomorrow, Mother?"

"I don't know why I wouldn't. I go ever Sunday, don't I?"

"Not every Sunday. Not when your stomach gets to bothering you too bad."

"Well, then, I guess I'll have to wait 'til mornin' to let you know. It's been botherin' me more and more here lately, seems like."

"Lord, I finally got that spoon out of that jam! I never thought I'd see the day when I did anything so foolish!"

"Good. I think I'm goin' in the livin' room and set down and work on this yarn for a while longer and see if I cain't make head or tails out of it."

"Maybe I can help you with it later if I can ever get this jam jarred up."

"Oh, pshaw, I give up, I'm never goin' to get this straightened out. I'm goin' out and see if the mail came yet."

"Well, I doubt if it would have come this early. Why don't you wait awhile instead of wearing yourself out walking out there over and over. Ruby will bring it in when she picks up theirs. She always does. Just wait a little while."

"Well, Law, I don't know what to do,"

"Just go sit in the living room and rest a little while, and I'll come in there and help you pretty soon,"

"I don't know if I'm goin' to need much more help from anybody for long."

"I just cain't get over how Jeanette done me at her wedding."

"What'd she do?"

"Well. I didn't get seated 'til almost the last thing."

35

"Now, Mother—who is the most honored guest at a wedding?"

"The bride's mother."

"OK, and when did they seat me?"

"Just before the Jeanette came in."

"All right. And when were you seated?"

"Not 'til just before you."

"All right then—"

"Oh—"

"Oh, here's Ruby coming with the mail right now, Mother."

"Good, maybe somebody finally thought about writin' to me for a change."

"Well, Lordy mercy, I did get a letter today."

"Good, Mother. I know a lot of people think of you all the time. They can't write every day."

"Well, I don't know about that. You're awful good to me, Minnie. You don't know how much I appreciate that."

"Well, all your kids are good to you. You know that. Bess wants you to come and see her all the time. You just don't want to go."

"Oh, Bessie lives away off down there in Pistol River now. It's a long trip."

"It isn't all that far. All you have to do is get in the car and ride along for a couple of hours."

"Somebody always has to help me in and out, and I have to set in the front seat. I cain't ride in the back seat of a car."

"They'll let you ride in front. Don't they always? Anyway nobody has forgotten you, Mother."

"Has Bertie Wilson lost her mind?"

"What?"

"I got a letter from Bertie yesterday, and here's another one, and it's just about word for word like the one that came yesterday."

"I don't know. Maybe she just forgot she'd already written to you."

"What in the world is the matter with her? I'm worried about her. It's just word for word."

"Oh, she's probably all right. But who knows? She is getting pretty old."

"Well, she's a lot younger'n I am."

"Yes, but people are different."

"Well, I cain't get over gettin' them two letters from her in a row. I don't know what in the world. She must be awful bad off."

"At least she's thinking about you, Mother."

"I guess she is, if she's thinkin' about anything. I think she's losin' her mind."

"Well, time will tell."

"Yes, it will. Always does."

"I wonder if there's a lot a apples comin' on this year?" said Grandma.

"Yes, I think there's a pretty good crop. It'll be time to make applesauce again pretty soon," said Mom.

"I'm looking forward to that," said Grandma.

REMEMBERING FREDDIE

4

We were the closest of the cousins, Freddie and I, because we grew up just across the road from each other, and neither of us had siblings in our age range. We each had a brother, 8 and 10 years older. Freddie's dad, Uncle Guy, was my mother's brother, eldest of her siblings.

We had each other and would drop in often since neither of us had phones then. I would go trotting a few yards down the road, then across and up the gravel driveway through the myrtle trees to Freddie's house, or he would come up to mine.

I had Toby, my Pekingese, and Freddie had Old Duke, but their companionship was limited so we needed each other as well. We needed somebody to ride with on the merry-go-round.

Our families frequently went places together—to the beach, the county fair and out on picnics. I always looked forward to Aunt Nota's deviled ham sandwiches that she made so lovingly as she seemed to do everything. They were delicious with a thin spread of butter, then a thin spread of deviled ham and cut diagonally very neatly.

Freddie and I were about three when we all went to the beach one time. Aunt Nota was worried about Freddie and cautioned him about going too far out into the surf. Mom told me later that I said, "Don't worry. I'll take care of him." He was four months older than I so they thought that was pretty funny. But I'm sure I would have.

Once we were in the grove behind our house, playing on the swing. We could have been around seven by then, and we got to talking about our looks. He ventured that "Oh, I think you're average-lookin" I said, "I think you're average-lookin' too." I think he was probably pretty generous in his assessment of me, and I probably could have done better for him; he was always a very cute little boy. Aunt Nota took extra care in combing his hair, dipping the comb in water several times during the process to help shape and perfect the nice wave in front just so.

They had a phonograph, a big wooden cabinet that you had to wind up with a crank. And they had two records. The only one I remember was Red River Valley. Sometimes he would play it for me when I was there. It seemed like a huge luxury to me to own one of those. We didn't have one.

We would sometimes go to Grandpa's and Grandma's place and run through the fields, down by the creek, fish a little maybe, with a homemade pole, a long stick with a string tied to it, and a hook tied on the end. I don't remember catching any fish. Certainly I didn't. My hook was usually caught in the brush along the edge of the water, any time I ever tried to fish. Sometimes we took along a lunch to eat among the birds and varmints, spending much of the day.

He was always ahead of me, and I don't really know

where we were going—just going I guess. I imagine Freddie was pretending we were out in the plains of the old west. I always followed, struggling to keep up, and sometimes got stuck at a fence that he had just gone over or through, and he would come back and help me get through, maybe by holding the barbed wire up so I could crawl under. Those were hot and tiring days, but a whole lot of fun. Freddie would often be explaining things to me or instructing me in some way.

He had a Little Orphan Annie decoder ring. He got it from the radio program, and would show it to me and explain how it worked and how you broke the code. It was always way over my head, but sounded pretty exciting. Or was it something to do with Ovaltine?

Once at his place, he built a bonfire and cooked us potatoes by peeling them very carefully and slicing them paper thin to fry. He explained as he worked, how you want them very thin because that's the way they are really good. And they were.

One year when we were in The Big Room at Valley View, probably 11, we decided we should make some money. So we went out when the Himalaya berries were ripe and picked gallons to sell. Mom took us to town at the end of each day where we knocked on doors and sold them all for $.50 a gallon, making $16 between us that summer, which we divided evenly. That suggests by my calculations that we picked 32 gallons during that season and felt very accomplished.

I don't remember ever having a cross word with Freddie. We got along perfectly, never got mad or irritated with each other—never once. We were the best of friends.

We grew up eventually and found our perfect spouses, going our separate ways. We were never estranged, just didn't stay in touch as much as we should have, living in faraway places, raising our own families. We both suffered huge losses in our lives, and enjoyed great rewards.

I still love fried potatoes, and I don't think I've ever cooked them without wondering if I'm slicing them thin enough, knowing I'm not, and feeling a little guilty, remembering Freddie.

I kind of yearn to run through a field again in the warm sun, and I'll bet he would like that too; maybe that's what he's doing now.

2011

ALLEGANY

5

After driving about 20 miles north of Coquille on Hwy 24 to Marshfield, we turned east up Coos River and headed to the logging camp just beyond Allegany, a little community with a post office and a school where we would live for about a year.

I thought I was in Snuffy Smith's neighborhood as the road was just like his. Sharp curves, one lane, with huge drop offs on the right down to the river, and cliffs going straight up on the left for much of the seven miles.

We were provided with a cabin to live in at the edge of the camp on a rise to the left of the road and below a hill of towering firs, behind it.

The cabin had one bedroom, and a large living room including a wood range that acted as a kitchen and provided warmth. Much like home in that sense. Maybe there was a little counter along the front too, near the stove. But no sink. The running water came from a faucet down toward the road, and we had to carry it up to the house in buckets. I think living there was a lot like camping.

We had no electricity. But you could walk right into the bedroom from the living room without going outside. I liked that. It seemed like a luxury to me. Except I didn't know the word luxury yet. I was four. Nor did I know hardship.

The cabin was furnished with a table and enough chairs to seat five people. I know that because Daddy's cousin Emmett Hammett boarded with us, there for supper on many days, and that made five people.

They also had bed frames, springs and mattresses in the bedroom. A double bed for Mama and Daddy and a cot for Boyd, and I think a crib for me. That's pretty old for being in a crib. But maybe it's all they had.

As usual, Mama got to work. On the old weather beaten shack, which had never seen paint inside or out. Daddy made an occasional trip down to Marshfield or Coquille for supplies and food and to check things out at home. Sometimes Boyd went with him, and once I did.

Mama ordered gallons of calcimine and a big brush and calcimined the whole inside of the cabin, which whitened the rough boarded walls and ceilings. She also obtained some red and white checkered cloth, put up curtain rods, and made curtains for the small-paned windows. She must have sewed them all by hand. There was no other option. She turned our shack into a cute little place.

The cabin sat on the level of an old logging road which extended out in front of the porch for several yards to the east where there was a large deciduous tree of some sort with a limb big enough to hold a swing. I always had a swing on one of the Improved Northern Spy apple trees at

43

home. And Daddy put one up for me on this tree here. So I had a place to sit and do my thinking.

One day on the swing, I decided to write a song. I was in a comedic mode, and thought a funny song would be good. I worked on it for quite a while and finally came up with this. Not quite satisfactory, but the best I could think of. "Old lady Jones—wanted her pipe—couldn't find it on a day like this—". It had a good tune though. That would be E—EEC—, E—EEC,—FFF-E-EED-D—C. I had a good audience—of two, I remember them looking a little quizzical when I sang it to them. But they chuckled a little. That was my first musical composition. And my last. Nobody knows it because it was never put down on paper. It was performed only once, and admitted to by the composer only now, reluctantly, 79 years later, when it doesn't matter. There's far more to be embarrassed by at this point.

A short walk up the hill through large Douglas firs, took us to the outhouse. I loved the pungent smell of the trees as you went through them. And their bark was blistered with sap that I liked to puncture with my thumb nail, and see it seep out. I learned that you can't wash that off; it's sticky. But you can easily get it off your fingers with just a little butter or Snow Drift, which Mama always had around for making pies and frying potatoes.

At the northeast front corner of the cabin, we had a rain barrel, mossy and fun for some reason. Maybe it was the popular song about it. Mama probably sang it to me.

"Oh, playmate, come out and play with me,
And bring your dollies three,

44

Climb up my apple tree,
Look down my rain barrel,
Slide down my cellar door,
And we'll be jolly friends—forever more."

I think we washed our hair with the water from the rain barrel. Somehow I learned that it is softer than other water and better for your hair.

Most of my daytimes during the dry weather were spent sitting in my swing, looking around outside, playing with Toby, and doing a little exploring nearby. In the summer it was fun to go down to the road and walk barefooted through the dust, which was several inches deep and felt as fine as baby powder or cake flour. There was little traffic on that road so it was a safe spot to play.

A few other children lived there too, and a few times I played with some of them. But not often. They were mostly a little older than me. I went to a girl's place once for a while, supposedly to play with her. She was jumping rope in the house, and would stop every once in a while to take a pill. She would say, "I have to take my pep pill." They were in a dish, and looked exactly like peanuts to me.

I told Mama about the girl jumping rope and about the pep pills. She was disgusted and told me "They were peanuts." Had I known that, I probably would have wanted one too. But it didn't bother me. I just never went there again. It wasn't an issue because I wasn't invited and I never thought about it.

Poor Toby. I petted him and played with him. He probably followed me around. But he never had a toy. There weren't dog toys in those days. I'd never seen a leash. Dogs were just on their own. That might have been better in his opinion. He never had dog food, just scraps of people food. I was his only friend. I don't know how good a friend I was. But I loved him. He was my only real friend up there.

One time I was sitting on the top step of the porch, in the sun. Toby was lying close by me. I reached over and petted him several times, trying to get him up to play with me. He wanted to sleep. I tugged on him, and he snapped and bit my hand. I was crushed. I bawled, loud enough that Mama came running out to see what was wrong. "Toby bit me," I wailed. She looked at my hand. "Why, he didn't even break the skin." By that time Toby had moved over and laid his head in my lap. "Look, he's telling you he's sorry. You're okay." I was. All that was hurt was my feelings for a minute. I've always remembered that sweet gesture, and the bite was just because I kept nagging him to play. I learned a little.

I had a jump rope while we were there too, and a big colorful rubber ball that we rolled back and forth with me sitting spraddle-legged on our big living room floor.

When it got dark, we lit the three kerosene lamps. There was plenty of room for me to spread out on my stomach and color in that big empty living room every evening by one of them. I'd have felt like Abraham Lincoln if I'd known about him.

Sometimes we went down to the splash dam and watched them dump the loads from logging trucks. That was always exciting. The logs were huge in those days, sometimes six or eight feet in diameter. Never less than three feet in my estimation, and they made huge splashes.

Other times we drove on up an even worse road, several miles beyond the camp to see the golden and silver falls, huge and spectacular in dense forest settings. We of course took a picnic.

The time I went home to Coquille with Daddy was during the Bandon fire in September 1936, which decimated the town, leaving only two buildings standing in the downtown. Bandon was 18 miles west by curvy road from Coquille, less as the crow flies. As we neared home, we saw charred snags of trees, and some were still burning on both sides of the road within sight of our house, just a few hundred feet away. But the fire never reached our place.

We moved back home soon after that.

I've always wanted a rain barrel ever since.

Mama always said that year up Coos River was the happiest time of her life. She felt so free.

MY SLOW BEGINNING

6

"The only useful thing I ever learned in school was that if you spit on your eraser it will erase ink." Dorothy Parker

When I turned 5, I was ready to go to school. But alas there was no preschool nor kindergarten around, and they had their rules. You had to be 6 or very close to it. So I put in a long, wasted year trying to entertain myself, mostly alone except for Toby, who was more like a terrier or a German shepherd than a lap dog, chasing away any big dog that might come around. I don't know if he was jealous or if he was trying to protect me.

There was no use in requesting early entry into school, and I wouldn't have met the challenge anyway, because I didn't know anything. I was pretty much a blank slate. I could count, but I didn't know one letter from another, and I still didn't know any more about that when I was old enough. They just had to let me in anyway.

They had always read to me at home, usually the same stories over and over—Little Red Riding Hood, The Three Bears, and other stories about living happily ever after.

Once my brother was reading to me. One story would end, and I would say, "Read that one," pointing to one of the illustrations. That went on for a while until he caught on and said in disgust, "You don't read the pictures; you read the words!" I didn't know that all of those marks were words, so I hadn't paid any attention to them. That opened up a whole new world for me and possibly was what triggered my burning desire to go to school.

Preparations were fun, going to buy school supplies every year—a pencil tablet, pencils, crayons, paste, scissors, and an eraser.

Just reading that list can almost put me into a sensual frenzy. Even now. They each had their own kind of smell and felt good. And we got some other things. Maybe a lunch pail and something to wear like new shoes.

The building, though a small country school, was well-built, and felt luxurious to me. The hardwood floors gleamed, and rows of child-sized wood and wrought iron desks on long runners, with seats that turned up, beckoned me to take a seat. I was entranced by the shiny white drinking fountains outside the classrooms, and the girls' restroom at the bottom of the stairs, furnished with rolls of white toilet paper, sinks with soap, and paper towels, very upscale compared to our outdoor facilities at home with a catalog. There was a playroom in the basement for rainy days, and outside 2 softball fields, swings, and a manually-driven merry-go-round filling the yard around the building.

I, and everybody else, loved to write on, and erase the smooth slate blackboards that covered most of the walls.

The first day of school we learned about the electronic

bell, which Mrs. Wilson, the big room teacher and principal, rang to call us in from recess and lunch, and to come in and take our seats in the mornings. We learned about raising our hands to get permission to speak or to get out of our seats for any reason, And about the cloak rooms, where we hung coats, stored galoshes and umbrellas, and shelved our lunches. There was no refrigeration nor kitchen facility so we had to bring our own lunch and drink every day.

The teacher introduced us to the library, a small room off the classroom, full of books she encouraged us to check out.

She taught us a game called Black Man, a form of tag where everybody was to avoid the "Black Man" who tried to tag someone else who then became the black man. We were all white. We never pictured an actual black man. Or at least I didn't. It was only years later that I thought about what that meant and how outrageous it was that the schools mindlessly taught it to us—in Oregon.

My teacher was Mrs. Cruise, a young-looking woman who always smelled powdery and flowery. She seemed nice.

Somewhat later I learned that teachers were real people like everybody else. I'd heard a lot about teachers but always thought they were some other entity, like an alien maybe. I had never thought the whole thing through, believing that they lived at the school. They were there when we came in the morning, there when we left in the afternoon, and seemed to own the place, so it stood to reason. I didn't know they ate and slept like the rest of us and had families and homes. I don't know how that eventually got cleared up for me.

I remember well the only academic activity we had that first day of school. The first graders were taught how to make a one, that is, a little straight vertical line. Then we were told to take out our new pencil tablets and to practice by filling up a whole page with ones while the teacher got the other 3 grades started on their work.

I pretty much had the concept of the one by the first 2 or 3 of them that I made, but I obediently filled up the page, feeling a little disillusioned about school. I had expected to learn to read. For me, I think some laziness settled in, which didn't serve me well as time went on and schoolwork became more challenging.

We had what they called "art" sometimes when we were provided colored construction paper and made something out of it by folding, cutting, and pasting, step by step, as instructed by the teacher, so that we ended up with identical works of "art".

We did a fair amount of coloring. I always had crayons and color books at home and had done plenty of that. I liked it. I was perfectly amenable to staying inside the lines, but I've never really figured out what is better about one side of a line than the other. The only redeeming feature about coloring, really, was that we got to pick our own colors.

I even saw that challenged in later years when I was counseling, by a teacher who picked up a boy's page and showed it to her class, using him as an example, derisively pontificating, "Look at this. Who ever saw anybody with blue hair!" Apparently she'd never heard of Picasso or Gauguin or Monet. I believe the kids that neglected to limit themselves to coloring only inside the lines and who picked the most unlikely colors, probably had the edge on creativity. I was obedient, and tried to follow directions, to my artistic demise.

People would always ask, "Do you like school?"

"Yes," I would say because I knew you were supposed to like it.

Mostly the things I liked were the new school supplies, recesses, lunch, the building, seeing the other kids, the blackboards, pencil sharpeners on the walls that magically made perfect points on the ends of yellow Ticonderogas, in contrast with the pencil sharpening we did at home, which was done by Daddy and his pocket knife. And I liked the muggy, soft, tan smell of the old, well-used Peter and Peggy primers we learned to read, the forerunners of Dick and Jane. Sometimes even the subject matter was interesting.

Ever since, I've always wished I could live in a school house with its blackboards, pencil sharpeners, and big oilcloth wall maps that you pull up and down like a window shade. Maybe that's why I always wanted to be a school teacher. Could it be that I still harbored, at some deep level, the belief that I could turn into one of those other entities who got to live happily ever after in a schoolhouse?

MY FIRST STAGE PERFORMANCE

7

In our neighborhood, Valley View School was the center for community events. They put on two programs each year, one at Christmastime and one at the end of the school year with graduation exercises. I remember some carnival events, Halloween parties, and pie socials in my early years.

My brother was in 5th grade when I was three, and our mother stayed in touch with the school. The teachers seemed like friends of the family, and she had them in for a meal sometimes. Miss Halliday was the first one I remember.

At home Mama read to me a lot, and when I was three, she taught me a poem. "I love my cow all black and white. She gives me milk with all her might." That's what I still remember. However it has to be Robert Louis Stevenson, and I recognize some of his other lines.

THE COW
(Robert Louis Stevenson)

The friendly cow all red and white
   I love with all my heart
She gives me cream with all her might
   To eat with apple tart.

She wanders lowing here and there,
   And yet she cannot stray,
All in the pleasant open air,
   The pleasant light of day.

And blown by all the winds that pass
   And wet with all the showers,
She walks among the meadow grass
   And eats the meadow flowers.

Mama must have changed it to a black and white cow because ours was black and white, to add a touch of realism for me.

We went to school one day where Mama and the teacher had me walk out and stand in a certain spot and say my poem. I didn't know what for though I imagine they told me I was practicing for a program, never mind that I didn't know what practicing meant nor what a program was.

Mama made all my dresses until I was grown, laying patterns on yardage spread out on the table and weighted in place with table knives as she cut around them and sewed up the pieces on her electric, White brand sewing machine.

She whipped up a blue and white milk maid's outfit for me, a blue dress with white apron and cap, and she'd found a shiny metal milk pail, my size, for me to carry. She got me all dressed, and we went to school to meet with the teacher and some other people where we'd been before, which I now know was backstage. We waited there for a while.

I didn't know why we were doing it, but then I didn't know why we did much of anything. I was just there, and people took me places. We'd done this before. I suppose Mama told me that we were going to the program, and I would say my cow poem for the audience. But if she did, I'm sure I didn't know what an audience was either.

I was told to go out where I'd gone before and say my poem, so I went out on the stage. But everything looked different. It was dark, and I saw all these eyes shining. A whole room full of glinting, beady eyes, staring at me. Silently.

I stood there for a while, wondering what this was all about. Then the teacher came out and said, "Go ahead. Say your poem now."

I thought about it. I almost did. I could have. I knew I should. But I didn't want to. She left me, I stood there thinking about it some more, starting to say it, and changing my mind several times until she came back again.

"Say your poem now." But there was something about this that I didn't like. I don't remember feeling stage fright, which I experienced many times thereafter. On reflection, maybe I felt exploited. And it took me by surprise. I think I felt tricked though I didn't have a word for it at the time.

They finally gave up and let me go back off stage. Without my saying a word, I'm sure to my mother's chagrin.

You can't win in that kind of situation. Seventy-nine years later, I still feel guilty for not doing what I should have, for disappointing my mother, and I suppose for making myself look foolish. But on the other hand I had my reasons.

I can still hear her, "Well, what do you know about that?"

All I know is that my first stage performance was a failure.

And it ended Mama's career as a stage mother.

LETTING GO AND HANGING ON TO FEARS

8

One of my earliest memories was of lying in my crib under the little casement window on the west side of the bedroom. The train track ran along the river at the bottom of the hill below that end of our house. I assume it came by every night. Many times I heard its soft chugging sound in the distance, getting louder and louder as it moved closer, and the mournful wail of its whistle at the crossing. By this time I was quaking because I thought it was going to come in the window and plow right through the house and me.

I remember feeling that I would like to tell somebody, but I couldn't. I don't think I could talk yet.

I wonder if that is the way animals feel when they try to warn people of dangers. Or when they have a serious need and can't explain it.

When I was a little older, I rode to town with Daddy one evening. He parked the Model A and went into the train depot to see somebody.

"Just sit right here and wait for me. I'll be right back. OK?"

Yes, I would wait.

I waited. It took a little longer than I would have

preferred. Daddy liked to talk quite a bit. That's when I heard a train in the distance. It got louder and louder and suddenly this towering black monstrosity went roaring past me. It was going to get me! We were parked right by the train tracks. I slid off the seat and crouched with my head down on the floor, to avoid the inevitable.

It took a second for Daddy to figure out where I was when he got back.

"What are you doing down there?"

"Train."

"Oh, the train can't hurt you. It's on a track, and it can't get off."

He tried to comfort me. And did. That problem was solved. Later my mother told me how bad Daddy had felt when he found me huddling in fear on the floor.

Surprisingly I grew up with an affection for trains. I was happy to learn that a track was in sight of my husband's and my first house in Alexandria, Virginia, and the train can be heard from my current house in Eugene. They still have a mournful wail, but I've always liked trains since I survived those early days.

I miss the picturesque choo choo trains we had when I was a child. Friends and I used to go down the hill to watch them go by, wave to the engineer, who always waved back, and wait for the little caboose, like a big oversized toy.

My early fear of trains has morphed into a more rational concern, which is that I still don't like the idea of being on a train track when one is coming.

And I've suffered plenty of stage fright, feeling half sick all day before a performance. You are scared to death they will throw rotten fruit at you, or boo. Or worse, just sit in silence when you give your funny lines. But there is something to be said for that. It gives you an edge; the scareder you are, the better the show.

There are times when you've done a performance several times; you could do it with your eyes shut; you're tired. You go through it, but it just doesn't quite reach the mark. So when I didn't feel nervous, I stood off stage before the curtain, and worked up a false stage fright, telling myself, "I'm going to forget my lines. I'm going to flop. They're going to hate me," breathing hard. I went on, and it gave me the edge I needed.

Fear is often a useful and necessary emotion. It can keep you safe.

Then there is the fear of people, of entering a roomful where everybody is going to be looking at you, and you won't measure up. I've always felt a little of that. But it was wasted energy because I've learned that everybody else is doing the same thing, thinking about themselves. Or at least they're not thinking of me. I'm just not that important.

And I, of course, share that biggest fear that most people have, that of speaking in front of people. I mean even asking a question in class or just making a statement. My mind goes blank before I get out what I wanted to say,

But I have a major fear, a phobia, which hasn't subsided, and I don't think it has any positive side. This one is hard for me to talk about as I'm required to say the word. That is, the name of what I'm afraid of. I can hardly write it or type it either. It is a fear of reptiles in general and

——OK——snakes (I said it) in particular.

As a young child I was fascinated by them, but never wanted to touch one. I think I can blame my mother who would hate to think she had caused this. But she screamed every time she saw one. I don't know if that caused it or if I was just born with the gene. It is a common phobia. But then many snakes are dangerous. All we had was harmless garter snakes. Not only are they harmless, they can be of benefit, eating pests that we don't want. But knowing that doesn't help. I went through my childhood hopping high through the grass, trying to avoid them whether I saw any or not. I wish them no harm. I just want them to stay away from me.

I've said it before. If I had to make the choice of being in a room with a wild lion or a baby garter snake, I'd pick the lion. If one of those reptiles got in my house, I'd have to move. Without my possessions.

This is irrational. Of course. That's what a phobia is— an irrational fear.

If I see a picture of one of these creatures in a magazine, I turn the page fast, am careful not to touch it, and throw away the magazine. When they're shown on TV, I change the channel.

Phobias can be cured. I learned how in my counseling training. I could teach anybody in a few minutes how to do that though it is a long boring process to carry out. But why don't I get the cure?

Because I might have to touch one.

And if I did that, I might suffer my demise before I'm ready.

"MY BROTHER WAS AN ONLY CHILD"

9

—was the title of a book by Jack Douglas that I can relate to.

So was my brother. He was 7 1/2 years older than me, and about the only thing we shared in common as children was that we walked the half mile to Valley View School for one year, more or less together, he swishing along in his cords, grumbling at me to hurry up as I trudged along behind through the gravel at the edge of the two-lane country road that led us to the school with two rooms and 8 grades. He was an eighth grader in the "Big room" as it was called. I was in first grade in the "Little room". The rooms were the same size. It was the kids who varied.

He was hoping for a brother when I was born. After he saw me he decided they should keep me anyway, they said.

I think I was a pain in the neck for my brother more than anything else. He was the good kid and the pretty baby, as evidenced by the big oval-framed picture of him hanging on the wall. He had jobs and responsibilities, appropriate for his age, such as milking the cow twice a day and carrying in wood for the kitchen stove, our one heat source. I might feed the chickens or pick some rhubarb or loganberries once in a while if nobody else had time. He was quieter and cooperative. I was the more active and bore watching, described as "always getting into things".

On my 3rd or 4th birthday my mother made little airplanes out of a stick of gum, some lifesavers, and a rubber band for party favors. After we ate the angel food cake and red Jell-O and the favors had been doled out, one was set aside on the little drop leaf table under an open window for my brother when he came home. I stood looking at that last little airplane, hardly able to resist it.

Shortly my mother noticed it was missing.

"What happened to Boyd's airplane? We just put it right here."

Being a rather creative child for three, or slow for four, I answered, "I was looking at it, and it just got up and flew right out the window."

My mother repeated that to others in the room, while trying to suppress the smile that kept creeping onto her face. They laughed. I was appropriately chagrined and never again tempted by thievery.

I was muscular for a girl, had big feet, pale skin, fine wispy hair, and my forehead was too high. My parents made the most of it though. My mother said a high forehead means high intelligence, and my father said big feet gave you a good understanding. Nevertheless, I always wore bangs, and heard frequent reminders to point my feet straight ahead.

My father, the barber for the family, in cahoots with my mother, shingled my hair up the back, which I didn't like. I wanted to look like Shirley Temple. I think it was a challenge for them to make me look halfway presentable at all.

They told me that when I was born, the doctor said I was a perfect baby except for had weak stomach muscles, which explained my protruding midsection until I was about 12 when things started to shape up a little better.

For years I was the only kid who wore long cotton stockings to school. They were held up by a complicated, uncomfortable harness and always bagged at the knees. My mother thought I needed the warmth.

Since I was prone to colds and croup I also went to school half the time with an old muslin dish towel, a cold wet end applied to my throat, the dry end wrapped around that, pinned in place with a big safety pin, and smelling like "Vicks Vaporub". To this day I don't know why. I was also the only one I ever saw who went to school with a rag around the neck.

When I was 5 they gave me a permanent. It resulted in a tight tangly curl that made the combing process long and nearly impossible every morning with loud complaining from me because it hurt. After that grew out, it was back to the shingle.

I had an older cousin, Glennis, who tried to help. She kept telling me to hold my stomach in. A younger cousin kept mentioning my Roman nose. She thought it was funny. I wasn't hurt, but it annoyed me because I couldn't do a thing about either condition.

My brother joined the Army Air Corps after he graduated from high school. He served in the South

Pacific—New Guinea, the Philippines, and Japan—and didn't return until the war was over when he was 22, and I was 14.

Our father died 4 months before he got home.

By that time I'd had a few years of piano lessons, he had a beautiful low tenor singing voice and liked to use it, so we started singing and playing together. He'd always sat by the radio on Saturday nights before leaving for the war, singing along with the Hit Parade, and knew every song. So we added popular music of the time to the hymns we knew and did a lot of music together for fun at home and for occasional performances. Sometimes I would harmonize with him, but mostly he sang and I accompanied.

Then 11 years after he came home, he walked me down the aisle.

And that's how two only children grew up and found out they each had a sibling.

LAWS AND GERTRUDE

10

They had funny names. And they were old. At least that's what I thought.

I was probably three or four. I didn't know exactly how we were related. I think Laws was Mama's cousin, Grandpa's nephew. "Laws" was short for Lawson, which I think is a nice name. But I didn't know that then. He was just Laws, which sounded like "loss".

A good-natured couple, Gertrude was friendly and plump, a motherly type though they had no children that I knew of. Laws had a slight build and was on the short side, Gertrude possibly a little taller. They seemed to like children.

Sometimes you live with memories that are so deep-seated that you hardly realize you have them. Only recently in my 9th decade, it entered my consciousness that I've regularly thought of Laws for all these years. He was telling once about a visit to the doctor who told him, "When you wash your hair," he demonstrated as if he were doing that, "scratch your head real good. Yep, he said to really scratch it all over." I realized I've never forgotten overhearing that, and I'm sure I've never washed my hair that I haven't thought of Laws. I don't know why, but I do.

Every time. It was just a part of me that I hadn't noticed.

I kind of wish if he was going to say something so memorable, that it could have been more profound, something I could aspire to that would make me a better person. But they were simple people.

During that short time they were around, they lived in a little cabin on Grandpa and Grandma's place, just north of their house. I often went to visit them when we were there. I would walk out Grandma's front door, across the porch and down the wooden steps, then turn left and wend my way past the two catalpa trees, one on each side of the gravel walk. These unusual trees had straight trunks and huge green leaves like elephant ears. They had foot-long beans that hung down all around after the blossoms faded, like big green icicles in the heat of summer.

Then I went through a part of the yard that seemed older and more wild than the English flower garden on the south side of the house where Grandma just stuck anything into the ground and it grew and flourished.

So I went through the deeper, browned grass and weeds, past Grandma's little "summer house", which was a wooden arbor with the peeling paint of age and the elements, square-topped with a pink rose climbing up the side, and with two opposing benches where cousins, Betty and Susan, and I used to go out and sit sometimes. It seemed like a romantic spot out of the past, and I've always wanted one.

Down to the left was the big weeping willow and Grandpa's woodshed with his whetstone sitting out in front of it. It was a wheel with pedals that turned it when he sharpened tools, scissors and knives. Just a little further on, the wild growth gave way to a little trail that led to Laws and Gertrude's door.

If it was mealtime they invited me to eat, and of course I did.

Once Gertrude told Mama, and Mama later told me, that they invited me to eat with them one day. She'd said, "We don't have much." That was a routine apology I suspect, for company. Then she told Mama, when we sat down to eat, I agreed, "You don't have much, do you?" She thought that was funny.

I never knew Laws to have a job of any kind while they lived there though my brother told me that Daddy had Laws and Grandpa help him sometimes in reaping the burls out of myrtle trees. That is the curly parts of the wood that make the most desirable accessories, a popular Coos County business. Daddy then cured and sold the burl. It was hard work, requiring using cross-cut saws, with one man on each end, and heavy lifting. It brought in a little income for them. But Daddy couldn't sell all the burls.

Like Grandpa, Laws never drove a car. One day before Christmas, he went to town to do his Christmas shopping. He walked the three-plus miles to town and back. He'd bought one present. It was for me. I don't remember the name of the little book, now long gone, but I remember I liked it, and in the top right corner was written in pencil, "5 cents". The price affected me not at all. I'm touched by that act though. It still means a lot to me.

It was a simple life they lived. There's something to be said for that. And I'm glad I got in on it.

GOING TO TOWN IN THE '30s

11

"Town" was Coquille, said to be named that after the Coquelle Indians, because it was the closest to the Indian word that the founders could think of. Some of the old-timers pronounced it Kokwell for years.

That's where we went when we needed to buy anything or needed entertainment, which pretty much consisted of going to the show. (That meant the "movies'.) Mom put the kibosh on bowling, probably because the bowling alley was on the wrong side of the tracks. That is, it sat next to the house of ill repute. But I didn't know there was one, or if I had I wouldn't have known what it was. I'm not entirely sure now.

We lived at Johnson Hill, 3 miles south of Coquille. Johnson Hill used to be owned by a man named Johnson who had a saw mill at the bottom by the Coquille River, and camp houses all the way up the hill. The gravel road went right by our land, down the hill, across the train tracks and on for a quarter mile along the river lined with old weather-beaten farm houses. By the time I was born, the mill was gone, but logging trucks rumbled down the road daily in a cloud of dust to dump their logs in the river where they were floated to Smith Woods Plywood Mill at

Coquille. Sometimes we went down and watched them, the enormous splash when a truck load of logs hit the water, the biggest thrill we could think up. Trucks often stood in line for our ongoing entertainment.

The old camp houses were owned or rented by other people who were our neighbors and friends by my time. Our unpainted garage and woodshed remained, and still stood the last time I was there. Our address was McKinley Route, Coquille, Ore. And we pronounced it, "rowt". If you forgot the route name, you could just write the name and Coquille, Ore., and it would be delivered anyway.

We went to town once a week or so, usually to William's Grocery store on Front Street, handed our list to Jess, the owner, who got an empty box and went around the small room, picking up the items for us. My mom, or dad, said, "Charge it," and we paid once a month. During the war years, I remember Mama pulling out her ration books and tearing out the stamps if she was buying sugar or Hills Brothers coffee.

Jess Williams was always a joker. Once when only one of an item was left on the shelf that was on Mama's list, he said, "Nooo, I can't give you that; I've only got one left, and somebody might come in and want it."

If we needed any kind of clothing or other dry goods, we went to Penny's with its shiny yellow and black tiles in front, and I got to watch them send the money up to the second floor by putting it in a container and pulling a chain which sent it flying up a wire. Shortly the change came down the same way. My cousin Betty and I both wanted to grow up to be clerks in Penny's so we could get to work that thing. Then the clerk wrapped your purchases in brown paper she tore off a big roll and tied it up with twine string for you to carry home. After I was in high school, Mom and I were known to go in and try on hats if we wanted a good laugh.

After I went away to college, I found a hat I couldn't resist so sent it to Mom as a gift for some occasion. It was covered with red cherries that bobbed and clinked together at every move. I knew Mom would get a good laugh at that. But she got me back, thanked me for the beautiful hat and wrote that she'd worn it to church last Sunday. I thought, "Oh, no, what have I done?" She got me.

Next door to Penny's was Slater's Variety store, a five and ten. We did much of our gift shopping there. I bought Daddy a little ash tray, made of pressed glass, shaped like a boat with a metal sail for Father's Day. And of course they carried Old Spice. I think Daddy got well-equipped with that. They had toys and books, and about anything you could think of except clothes and groceries. After I got to be about 12, cousins, Susan, Bette, and I bought Pond's cold cream, Jergen's Hand Lotion, and Tangee lipstick, the kind with a neutral color that changed according to your body chemistry to match your coloring. They said.

And later Tabu cologne and bath powder, the rage. At home we had a number of things, like pretty little vases, pitchers, or cactus pots that Aunt Nota, Aunt Eunice, or others had given Mama or me for Christmas, that had been purchased in Slaters.

Folsom's Grocery was across the street by the Pastime Tavern and Lorenz dry goods. But Lorenz was more expensive than Penny's so we never went there.

Nearby sat the little meat and fish market with its white tile floor which extended out to the sidewalk, along with a fresh smell of the sea, evident even when just walking by. At the end of the block was the Liberty Theatre which had mostly cowboy shows, Shirley Temple movies, and comedies with The Three Stooges or Joe E. Brown.

Bonney's drug store sat around the corner, down the street from the old Coquille Hotel, which later opened up the Chenango, a nicer restaurant with an old-west name. On that same street was The Sentinel office, the weekly newspaper, and a music store which sold mostly sheet music, but for some reason had a beautiful Heisey glass salad bowl in the window for $5 which Mom took a shine to, but never imagined she'd have at that price. Daddy bought it for her birthday. She'd been known to get a flashlight or a spade for presents, so I believe the bowl was one of her more cherished possessions. It's still in the family.

Bill's Place, an old, Men-Only saloon with brass rails and spittoons was at the end of Front Street on the other side of the town brothel, next to the barber shop. Of course I've never seen the inside, but it is now historic. Later the Casino, another tavern, went in on Front Street, maybe trying to keep some balance with the proliferation of churches in town.

We went to the Emmanuel Baptist Church. At the other end of the block was the Episcopal, a block another direction was the Christian Scientist Church. And nearby the Methodists. Beyond that were the Christian, the Four

71

Square, Nazarene, Seventh Day Adventist, and Catholic churches. Those are the ones I remember. I thought the Bible Belt was down South until I looked back at Coquille in later years. About half of Coquille was populated with displaced Arkansawyers anyway, but most of them were Baptists and many of them my relatives,

There was a bank, a post office, and a tiny telephone office building, still standing in 2013, where my mother was an operator before she was married in 1921. The operators answered a lilting, "Number please", and plugged you in. If you wanted to know anything, you could pretty much ring the operator and ask. Kind of like a flapper-era audio precursor to going online for information.

Other places opened over the years, like The Bootery for shoes, Mode O' Day for dresses, and The Roxy, a newer, fancier movie theatre which cost you fifty-five cents for a ticket instead of the quarter you paid at the Liberty, and specialized more in musicals and epics. There was a bakery, Farr's Hardware that has probably been there a hundred years, still open in 2013, and The White Cottage, a little cafe down on Front Street where we used to go for chili and chocolate milk when we were in high school. Brandon's soda fountain near Penny's remained popular with teenagers as well.

No matter where you wanted to go in town, you could park almost anywhere and just take a short walk to any of these places because they covered only a few blocks. And when you did, everybody spoke to everybody else they passed on the street whether they knew them or not. When I went out to the University of Oregon, I remember it being

72

this way on campus too. Or maybe it was just me. But it makes sense, because the regular students at that time numbered almost the same as the population of Coquille. Four thousand.

Of course in Coquille you had to do all your trading during the six days stores were open. Everything was closed on Sundays. I believe the general consensus was that it was a sin to buy anything on Sunday, and it was a sin to work Except for housewives of course. You had to have your big Sunday dinner. The Sunday Christians ran things. The Adventists just had to make do. You couldn't get a box of salt if you ran out on Sunday. So there was some borrowing from house to house.

Coquille still has just under 4000 people. It has a high school, junior high and grade school. The long time plywood mill has been razed, though there is still a saw mill or two around. Safeway and McKay's Market came in. William's and Folsom's groceries are long gone. The Liberty and Roxy are gone. Many of the churches still exist. Some have moved or rebuilt—bigger if not better. The community building, built in 1942, entertained touring concert series and held dances with big bands such as Woody Herman through the forties while I was in high school, and it still stands.

My brother who, in 2014 at age 90, still lives at Johnson Hill in a house he built in the early 50's, just a few yards from the one where he was born, says "You can't buy a pair of sox in Coquille anymore."

TEA CUPS AND COFFEE POTS

12

Tea cups at our house were used for more than just tea. Or coffee.

The smell of fresh-brewed Hills Brothers woke me every morning in my early years. I didn't drink it, but it had a heavenly, rich fragrance that filled the house, the way Mama brewed it, nice and strong, in her little pot-bellied aluminum percolator that stood on the back of the wood stove, crackling and popping, providing the heat.

I was in my thirties before I started drinking coffee, and that was only because it was always available, socially acceptable, and non-caloric. But it never tasted as good as Mama's smelled. And since it was more palatable when accompanied by something sweet, other than my husband, like a cinnamon roll or cookies, the non-caloric aspect probably never did anything for me.

I think I learned about saucering from Grandpa, or maybe it was Daddy. He did it too when the coffee was too hot to drink. I think it was only the men who saucered their coffee. It was a common practice in those days—enough that it was given a name. But Daddy always kind of laughed when he did it as if it was a little odd, or crude.

Maybe Mama didn't quite approve. It couldn't have been socially acceptable behavior when you were in good company. They just poured a little out of the cup onto the saucer to cool, and slurped it from the saucer. You also saw men doing that in restaurants sometimes.

That reminds me of another custom in those days. Men often whiled away their leisure time, whittling. They would sit outside on a stump or a rock with a piece of wood and a pocket knife (All of them had one of those.) and whittled, sometimes making something recognizable like a toy gun or a paddle. Daddy often did that. Well, there wasn't any TV to entertain you. We had a radio, but we turned it on only at night. Some whittling produced artful results.

We had some other pastimes when we were together, like playing Authors or Old Maid, checkers or Chinese checkers. Nothing too sophisticated. For Chinese checkers, I think we each had our own color. The only one I remember was that Daddy always had orange. Mama probably had yellow because that was her favorite color. I didn't have a favorite yet, and I don't imagine Boyd did either. I think we had a living room by the time we got Daddy the Chinese checker game. And I seem to remember that we always put it down in the middle of the living room floor and played from there, the four of us huddled around it on our hands and knees, on the new wine-colored wool rug.

Tea cups had a couple of other uses at our house. When we washed our hair at the kitchen sink, we poured some Ivory Flakes into one, added water, and left it to stand a while. It became a gelatinous consistency, and you just dipped some out with your fingers to use as shampoo. My hair seemed to have more gloss and body in those years before I started buying Prell. Mom's explanation, "It's that detergent," referring to the Prell. We had a bias against detergents when they came out. I'm not sure that she ever got over it. Maybe I should go back to the Ivory Flakes. When Mama baked, she always measured the flour and sugar in a tea cup because she never owned a measuring cup. Then she used silverware, the teaspoons and tablespoons, to measure the baking powder, salt, and soda. Somehow things always came out pretty well, in fact perfectly for my taste.

Once Daddy and I went shopping to buy Mama a present. He was thinking about a standing electric mixer. One of those big things with several bowls that you could just measure ingredients into, turn it on, and let it do the work. Wouldn't that have been nice. But I saw a shiny aluminum tea kettle that could replace her old black cast iron one. It looked so much nicer to me. And so modern. Daddy let me decide.

Mama got a new tea kettle. It probably heated water almost as well as the old one. She continued to beat egg whites with an old egg beater or a whisk, and beat cake batters by hand. (That incident is probably one of the most representative ones of my whole life—making dumb decisions and feeling guilty about it for the rest of time.) And she continued to measure the flour and sugar in a tea cup.

On gift-giving occasions I don't know why it never occurred to me to get Mama a measuring cup or measuring spoons. I was always trying to find something pretty for her. Practicality and making her life a little easier never occurred to me.

I wish I could go back just long enough to make some changes.

I'll bet there aren't many people who can imagine how sentimental a person can get, over thinking about tea cups, Hills Brother's coffee, an old aluminum percolator, and their mother always having to make do while the men saucered and whittled.

A MYRTLE TREE, A PIG, AND A MAN

13

"In the morning of today part way to school I met a glad surprise. There was my pet pig waiting for me. I gave him three joy pats on the nose and did call him by name ten times. I was so glad to see Peter Paul Rubens."——Opal Whiteley

We lived in the middle of the myrtle trees, we always had a pig, and we had several tenants in our service station after Daddy quit running it.

Virgil and Iva McKinney, with their little girl, Raydean, rented it for several years. They were a nice, Seventh Day Adventist family. Iva was a wonderful cook, and I think she took the lead in their faith. Virgil went along, maybe partly because of the good and abundant food. He was a husky, macho type who drove trucks. He was a little dense, though a good guy, and he tried to be helpful.

Once Mama made the mistake of commenting in Virgil's presence, that she was afraid the old maple tree behind our house could fall or break off, and she thought it should be taken out before it hit the house.

A few days later we came home from somewhere, and

were shocked to see—no, not that the maple had been cut down and fallen on the house, to our good fortune—but that an old myrtle tree, a distance from another end of the house, had been cut to the ground, lying like a fallen soldier. I felt like I'd lost a friend. My eyes welled as I gazed at that beautiful tree, lying there, forsaken.

Virgil was trying to do us a favor. But he didn't know a rotten old maple from a vigorous lovely myrtle. Even I knew that.

Another time when he helped us out, I will never forget.

We had some livestock. A milk cow, chickens, and a pig. At some level I knew that the pig was raised to be eaten. He lived in a pen, big enough for him to turn around, walk a few steps, lie down to sleep, and eat slop. It was basically open to the elements but with sides and a roof. I fed him sometimes, by carrying a bucket of food scraps and I don't know what else mixed in, and pouring it into his trough. He always oinked at me. But I was too stupid to respond. I think he was smarter than me.

One day Mama said, "Daddy's down trying to fix the pig pen before the pig gets out. It started falling apart." I walked out to see what was happening, and felt sorry for Daddy. It looked like a big job to keep the pig in and hammer the pen together at the same time. But I also felt sorry for the pig, trying to get free.

He had lived in that confined space, entirely alone, for his whole life.

One time I've never forgotten was when I emptied the bucket a little too fast, and some of it splashed in his face, dripping off his nose. He oinked. It looked like he felt a little embarrassed, blinking his eyes. I felt bad, but I laughed at him, like a bully. I should have apologized. I thought about trying to clean it off but had no way to do it that I could think of. I felt sorry, but he didn't know it, and I walked away, back to the house.

Daddy was working on getting the pen back together when I saw that the pig had gotten out. And then, I was surprised. He started to run. I didn't know he could. He took off across the field, out in the sun, running with the wind. I knew he shouldn't be doing that, but he looked so happy. Ecstatic. I thought I saw him smile.

Virgil ran into his house, and came back out with his rifle, aimed it—I yelled, "No!"— He fired. He was a good shot. The pig fell. In the middle of his first taste of freedom—the first, few-second-run of his life. I realized, too late, that I loved that pig.

That's the way it was done in those days. Many of the neighbors had a pig too. I was spared the butchering process, as always.

We ate him I'm sure. But that was a separate thing. I didn't make the connection.

I am so sorry I never befriended our pig. I could have talked to him, named him, brought him an apple, but I didn't because I never thought of it. I regret that I never petted him. My grief and my long memory of our pig didn't help him a bit.

There's a lesson to be learned.

"Peter Paul Rubens did have going with me three times on searches, but today the pig pen was fixed most tight. I

couldn't unfix it with a hammer so he couldn't go with me. Today I did go on, and did come back to give him more goodbye pats on the nose."——Opal Whitely

.

TAKING TRIPS IN THE DEPRESSION

14

Every year my family took a trip. Usually it was around Oregon, up to Astoria, over to central Oregon, or down to Curry County. Once we went into California, and once to Idaho where relatives lived.

The first car we had in my lifetime was the Model A Ford, which had the uga uga horn and little isinglass window vanes on the sides. And they had running boards that you could sit on when it was parked. You sometimes had to give them a crank to get them started. I remember Mama or Boyd inside the car, having to work the spark up and down sometimes while Daddy was outside cranking. When it started, he would run back and jump in the front seat, and work it again to keep it alive before we pulled out. No heaters in those days, no car radios, nor CD players. The cars were drafty with hard seats, so we had to dress warm.

They had hotels then, but we always stayed in tourist cabins—in our price range. This required taking along bedding—sheets, pillows, and quilts, because all they supplied were iron bedsteads with thin mattresses on the springs. Once I remember Mom, horrified, thinking she saw bed bugs. At least in these modern times, we didn't have to share beds with strangers, the way it was not so many years before, out west anyway as I've been told.

They also had kitchen facilities, but supplied no equipment, so we had to take pots and pans, utensils, dishes and flatware, cups and bowls, a dishpan and soap, dishrags, dish towels, wash cloths, and bath towels for whatever cleaning up we could do without a bathroom. That wasn't particularly a problem, not unlike home.

And of course we had to take along a big cast iron skillet for frying the potatoes and making pancakes. The food. Cans, jars, and bottles of this and that, a big bag of potatoes, sacks of sugar and flour, salt, and other staples. It was almost like moving your whole household every day. We didn't have much furniture so there wasn't much left at home when we took these trips.

I don't know how we got it all in the car, and how it held us as well, but I remember being packed pretty snuggly in back with my big brother among the boxes, bags, and rolls of this and that.

We seldom, if ever, stayed more than one night in one place, so that meant unloading everything, cooking, making beds, cleaning up, and reloading every morning. I don't know how we did anything else. In fact that is the main thing I remember about most of our trips, just staying in the cabins. And I always felt a little homesick—for the cabin, each time we left one.

My mom must have been worn out, doing all this stuff that would have been a lot easier at home. I never heard her complain though. We had fun just enjoying the change of scenery and adventure. And Daddy helped out. He always fried the potatoes.

We somehow fit in some sight-seeing too. I remember the redwoods in Northern California, the tumble weeds in central and eastern Oregon, the Sea Lion Caves on the Oregon coast, the fish hatchery on McKenzie Highway, the lava beds, and the observatory overlooking them on the Santiam pass, from our various trips.

Now and then we ate in a cafe. That was only because we were occasionally too far away from the cabin to get back to cook. And we ate only one thing in public eateries—hot dinner sandwiches, beef or turkey on white bread with mashed potatoes, all smothered in gravy. We weren't there to try out the local cuisine. It was probably the most you could get for the money. We were all fine with that. I'm not sure I knew you could get anything else in a restaurant at the time. Even now, in the 21st century, if you want to revisit that adventure, just go to the Busy Bee or Fins Drive-in in Springfield, Oregon.

This was also the case at home. Eating out was not in our repertoire. Nothing you did for recreation in our family. It was only in the case of need. My parents never went out for a meal. The only time Mama didn't have to cook was every Sunday evening when Daddy did his fried egg sandwiches and cocoa, or when we were at somebody else's house and they invited us to eat. Feeding each other was always spur of the moment, not by invitation. Most of us didn't have phones, and nobody of our acquaintance wrote a note saying "Come to our house on Tuesday for supper at six." If you showed up at lunchtime or suppertime, you usually got fed.

I think we gave more than we received on that score. There was a period of time when Daddy's cousin Emmett Hammock and his wife Perna and five kids had moved away, but came back every weekend, and headed for our house first. They showed up every Friday at about five. Perna always called out good-naturedly as she came in the door, "Is dinner ready?" It always was. Nearly. As soon as Mama added another pile of potatoes to the pot, and opened a few more jars.

That got to be tiresome for Mama. She wanted to put a stop to it after months of overwork. I think it ended only when we moved to Allegheny. Even then, Emmett, who was also working up there, took his board with us, coming for supper every night. Just one extra was no problem. Except it was a little frustrating to Mama and Daddy when we had Chinese noodles, and he refused to try the soy sauce, which Daddy called bug juice. "Emmett, just try this. You'll like it." "No, I'm all right without it."

On one trip to Central Oregon, we were getting home late, and stopped at a place along the road for food. They had baked ham sandwiches, and it seemed that was the only choice. So we took them to the car and ate as we drove on. Daddy complained about their outlandish cost. Forty-five cents apiece! "Highway robbery." In those days, a sandwich commonly cost a dime. And then he grumbled about the fact that there was nothing on them but butter. "No lettuce, no tomatoes, no cheese, no nothing. Forty-five cents!"

I said nothing, but happily ate my sandwich and took note that a ham sandwich with nothing but butter, is the way to make them. It was delicious. I don't eat pigs now. But if I did that's the way I would make a ham sandwich.

Actually, years later in France, with my husband, Mel, the kids, my mother and Mel's parents, we stopped on a crisp early morning at a cafe which suggested—what else? Ham sandwiches. That seemed to be all they had available at the time, the first time I realized that backwoods Oregon isn't so different from sophisticated France. So that's what we had with big mugs of hot cocoa.

The sandwiches were French baguettes, split lengthwise, filled with baked ham, and cut in half, ending up in foot long sections, which dwarfed my 4-foot-10-inch mother-in-law. There was nothing on the bread. Not even butter. Just bread and ham, and amazingly, it was delicious. I don't know what they cost. But I wondered what Daddy would have thought. Probably pretty much as he did that night going home. But they were perfect for a cold, foggy morning.

This was before the days when France gave in to some American ways, began to offer mayonnaise and all sorts of other American style accoutrements on sandwiches, and opened McDonald's around the country.

When we drove the Model A down the driveway at home after our annual trip, we had to unload and get everything inside. We didn't lock the doors in those days, and Mom would say, "I wonder who's been here," as we went in. Somebody usually had. Some relative or neighbor. They might have left a box of fruit on the table, or something else they had that we might like. They just went in and put it down. "Looks like Cince and Eunice were here," they'd say," or "Spud and Irma "or "Guy and Nota."

Those weeklong trips were one of the fondest memories I have of those early years. In spite of a little grumbling from Daddy, just that once. We all had a wonderful time. There's a togetherness families have when they're on a trip that it's hard to have in any other setting or occupation. I don't know if you could call this a luxury, traveling in our style. But we were lucky to be able to go anywhere in those days. And the memories it created are priceless.

MRS. FOX

15

When we got the piano, we decided I would take lessons. Mom found Mrs. Fox, a piano teacher in Coquille. We bought the red First Grade John Thompson's Modern Course for the Piano from the music store, and I started my new career.

I was eight. Beginning by learning Middle C, I learned the names of all the keys on the keyboard, the notes on the staffs, rests, the clef signs, sharps and flats, and a new piece each week. Simple though they were, I felt some satisfaction. I was a mediocre practicer. But I learned to play one new piece a week.

Occasionally Mrs. Fox had all her students come in on a Saturday when she tried to teach us some of the rudiments in a back room with a big blackboard. I got a little out of that, but not much. I imagine I was the youngest, or one of the youngest in the group. Plus the others were probably all town kids as they seemed to know each other. And they seemed smarter and way ahead of me.

I never felt particularly well-liked by Mrs. Fox from the time I had to ask her to call my Mom at my aunt's house where she waited while I had my lessons, to let her know when to come after me.

Around the holidays she invited all her students to dinner one evening. There were eight or ten of us, and everybody was scurrying around busily helping her get the food together and on the table. Except me.

It was a little scary to me; I felt out of my element. I was kind of standing there, as usual, not knowing what to do. There were stacks of plates and piles of silverware on the sideboard. She suggested that someone could set the table and decided that would be a good job for me. It was fine with me as my mother had taught me the proper way to do that, the knife on the right with the cutty side facing the plate, the spoon right of the knife, and the fork to the left of the plate. I did that all the time at home. So I did it with no problem and stood around some more. Then she noticed it wasn't finished.

"I thought Jeanette was doing that," she intoned. I thought I had. But no. There was another pile of forks. All we ever had at home was one fork apiece. We'd never set the table with a row of forks. So one of the more able and knowledgeable students finished the job while I stood there—abashed.

I was reminded of that experience several years ago when I was working at Bill Medford Real Estate and our office was honored as Real Estate Office of the Year by the Chamber of Commerce with a lovely, formally-presented dinner. Bill and Bev, co-principal brokers, got up to express appreciation, and Bill, who had grown up in Oklahoma, in his inimitable fashion, announced, "If any of you're short of forks at your table, we've got a lot a extras over at ours."

At Mrs. Fox's I was seated to her left, so everything was passed to me first. I'm surprised she didn't have someone serving us from the left and taking away from the right. But as it was, I had to know what to properly do with the varied items of food and wondered what that little plate to the left of mine was for.

We'd also never used bread and butter plates at home, so I merely suspected that's what they might be. But I couldn't watch what anybody else did because I was first. I passed on the bread, and observed how others were doing it because I expected to be corrected if I put something in the wrong place. Good thing she didn't have finger bowls. I probably would have drunk the contents.

I did learn that night about bread and butter plates and multiple forks. And that you pass the food to the left. I always remembered that.

However recently when my family was discussing that issue again, as we tend to do at every meal and then go ahead and pass it all directions anyway, Christy informed me that the rule is—to the right! She is correct! I looked it up.

And I had to suffer through that dinner because Mrs. Fox didn't know that simple rule!

Another time we had a little recital at her house where my piece was a duet with her. About halfway through, my nerves got the best of me, and I hesitated on a note. Instead of adjusting to me, she went ahead and finished the whole piece by herself and then said, "Why did you stop?" in front of everybody, no doubt embarrassing my mother.

So I was well-established as the weakest link in the

group. But I never complained. I just felt a little sick to my stomach on lesson days.

I stuck it out for three years. When I'd gone through the Third Grade book, we decided I would take a break. But I didn't quit playing. I started enjoying it more actually, and it became my route to relaxation and pure pleasure. I learned more when I wasn't taking lessons than when I was. If I felt bothered by anything, I went to the piano and cheered myself up. It also helped my self-esteem as I was more in demand, and felt I had some skill.

I had never actually learned to read time, at least not by sight as I played. I knew what the various notes meant however couldn't apply it on a new piece without counting it out first.

I started babysitting when I was about eleven and spent my earnings buying sheet music for popular songs. Knowing how the songs went, helped me learn to read time, in a backwards approach. Anyway most of that music was more fun playing and singing than most of the little pieces in John Thompson. Soon I began to play at school for our Friday singing, and shortly for church.

I took a few more years of lessons from Bobby Burns when I was in high school and began to accompany singers at assemblies and the girls' chorus classes. Mr. Withnel, the chorus teacher approached me, expressing a concern after I'd played for Lila Danielson, with a beautiful soprano voice.

"You're the accompanist, so you follow the lead of the singer! You don't take the lead," said Mr. Withnel. "Take a musical breath when they do, and come in again when they do." My eyes were opened. I was the "trained" musician so I'd always followed the directions in the music. When it said accelerando, I speeded up. When it said ritardando, I slowed down, and I got louder when it said crescendo. No matter what the singer was trying to do. She just had to follow me.

It took five minutes, and I had a whole new approach. It worked. I loved accompanying more than anything else about playing after that. Even Bobby Burns heard me later and complimented me on being one of the best accompanists in town. Of course that was Coquille. I was probably one of very few in town.

I went on to major in music at the U of O, accompanied singers, and taught it in public schools for a number of years. I was no virtuoso, but I was proficient.

I was the only one I know of Mrs. Fox's students in those years who went on with music. It has been a huge part of my life. I'm sure she never thought I, of all people, would, and probably never knew I had. That's all right with me.

But I do wish, now that I know, that I could let HER know that it is HIGHLY improper, and no self-respecting person would EVER—pass to the left! ALWAYS pass to the right!

ME AND THE TELEPHONE

16

For all of my growing up years, in the 30s, 40s and 50s, we never had a phone. Mom wouldn't have one. Either she found it annoying or too self-indulgent, probably both. She wasn't much for putting on airs. She had actually been a telephone operator before she got married and seemed to have enjoyed the job saying she quit only because my father said, in keeping with the times, that, "My wife is not going to work." I think she wondered when that was going to happen. I never noticed her enjoying much leisure time.

That was in the days when you had to make a short ring to reach the operator who answered a musical, "Number Please," and you told her the number you wanted to reach. She would pull out several long wires, crisscross them, and plug them in to connect you.

My grandmother and several other relatives and neighbors got phones. I think they felt proud of having such a modern convenience.

I never talked on a phone until I was 8 or 9, that time at Mrs. Fox's house.

"You can call them yourself," she said tersely.

"I don't know how," I said meekly.

"Don't know how to use a phone? It's high time you

did." She seemed genuinely shocked that anybody could be that backward.

I was shaking in my oxfords. Her phone was black, shiny, and daunting. She made me do it though, and I somehow got it to ring. I must have said something though I just about lost my voice as my throat closed up from stark fear. They probably thought, "That must be Jeanette," because Mom soon showed up to pick me up.

The phones in the country, where I lived were those big oaken boxes which hung on the wall with a cone-shaped receiver on one side, a cone to speak into, and a crank on the other side that you had to turn to make it ring. You could ring anybody on your party line directly by making the correct combination of long and short rings. You had to turn the crank several times in succession for a long, and make a quick jerk for a short. Grandma knew every ring on her line. When she heard it ring she would stop and listen. "I wonder who's calling Eunice," she'd say. Then she might well go pick up the receiver and listen, to find out. "Oh, that was just Verna calling to see if Eunice was coming to town today."

There were some frustrations with owning a phone in those days. Somebody might be on the line when you wanted to make a call, and you had to keep checking to find out if they were off yet. Or somebody else might be listening in to your call, or they would keep checking to find out if you were done yet. Sometimes somebody would just break in and tell you in no uncertain terms that they wanted the phone. There seemed to always be one long-winded person that hogged the line.

Maybe that is why Mom never wanted a phone. It was just too much of a hassle, and I know she didn't approve of her mother listening in to calls.

When I had moved back home and was teaching at Myrtle Point High School, I met a nice-seeming young man who asked for my phone number. Almost everybody had one by then. I had to tell him "I don't have one." He didn't believe me of course. I added that he could call me at the school and I would call back. He wasn't interested. I'm sure he thought I had a husband or some arrangement at home that he didn't want to get involved in. So my style was somewhat cramped.

After that I became engaged and decided that planning a wedding by long distance was too impractical, having to borrow phones continually. So I had one installed in my mother's house whether she wanted it or not. She didn't complain too strenuously, and even warmed up to it eventually, coming to enjoy talking to her sisters regularly.

Fast forward:

Now I have 3 cordless phones, convenient to anyplace in the house, and a cell which usually hides out in the bottom of my purse, is downstairs when I am upstairs, or is run down when I, like a cat on the prowl, try to give it a call so I can track it down. Of course it is now illegal to talk on it while you're driving. I was given a Bluetooth so I can, except that the phone I have won't work with a Bluetooth, and I would have to pay a big fine to Verizon to get one that would. So the Bluetooth goes back to Costco—if it isn't outdated yet.

I believe we are now in what will be called The Wire

Age. There are 42 wires running from the wall to the power strip, from the power strip, to the answering machine, to the computer, the FAX machine, the scanner, the printer, a modem, and a couple of speakers, preventing any hope of ever vacuuming under or around the desk again. It's almost the same by the television set which is wired to a DVD player, a VHS player, a high fidelity sound system, four speakers, a receiver box, and several unidentified boxes, requiring 3 remotes if you are going to use all of that.

I got into "bundling" with QWest. That means that your home phone, your cell phone, the internet, and the TV are all billed together, everything is much simpler, and you get a discount. Turns out QWest doesn't know a thing about Verizon that you have to use for your cell phone, or Direct TV that you have to use, so you have to call those companies directly if you have a problem with them. Except, they keep their phone numbers a secret. All of these are on the same 12-page bill, undecipherable to me. Maybe if I went for a PhD. It's about like trying to pay your taxes.

The phone service includes voicemail, call wait, unlimited minutes, unlimited long distance, and free directory assistance, which I've used a lot because you can't find numbers in the phone book anymore. My phone bills started going up. Turns out they changed their minds about directory assistance and don't offer it anymore but didn't bother to tell anybody. They now suggest you get on the internet for numbers. What if you don't have internet? There are still some holdouts like my mother and the telephone, who don't have one, but still like to use their phones.

Have you ever tried to call a phone company? They don't seem to like using the phone. When you reach them and have pressed all the right buttons as instructed, a robot asks, "Please enter the number you are calling about, beginning with the area code. Why do they do that? You enter it and then push all the buttons again. When you finally get a real person, the first thing they say is, "What is the number you are calling about, starting with the area code?"

"The one I just entered," you want to say. Next time I'm going to just make up a number when I enter it, to see if anybody notices.

"How may I direct your call? If you are a QWest customer, press 1; otherwise press 2. For repair press 3; for customer service press 4," And so it goes. Once you've pressed enough buttons for them, you get the next automaton who tells you another series to press, and then the music comes on or a person yakking about how wonderful their service is. Uh huh. Then you get a real person, but it's the wrong department, so you press some more buttons or they transfer you several times, you get cut off about then, and go through the whole process again if you're up to it, and finally you get a real person— in North Carolina, with a foreign accent that you can't understand, and they can't understand you.

The last time I tried this, I told the person that I am on the Do Not Call list, but I keep getting calls that I'm not supposed to be getting. "May I put you on hold for a moment?" After several minutes, he came back and said,

"Yes, you're on the Do Not Call list."

"That's what I just told you," I'm tempted to say.

I explained that I had followed a recent unwanted call by dialing Star 69. It gave me a number, but it was for a legal office in Illinois who told me that they get other calls like this, so their number is obviously being given out in error by the phone company.

The QWest person said, "Well, why don't you just call them and tell them to quit calling you?"

I said, raising my voice, "Because I don't have their number; I was given a wrong number for them. That's my problem." I enunciated slowly and clearly, repeating my story which he still didn't understand. So I asked him who enters the numbers for Star 69, which they claim tells you the last number that called you, thinking maybe I could call them directly for some help.

"Oh, no that's automatic,"

"Somebody must put those numbers in there," I said.

"No, that's automatic," he answered, "We don't have anything to do with that."

"You mean it's handed down from above? And it's still wrong? No human on earth has anything to do with it?" My voice rose even higher in spite of my attempt to stay calm. I felt like a female Louis Black, shaking in frustration.

I took a few deep breaths, and said a heartfelt thank you, and goodbye.

He quickly asked if he could help me with anything else.

"No, I don't think so."

He worked in a quick request before we hung up. "If

anybody from QWest calls you about how you would rate this call, tell them I was a one—a ONE. That will help."

That was so pathetic, I began to feel a sense of warmth toward this person. I wanted to help.

In short, I'm sure glad in this enlightened age that we don't have to put up with those old party lines any more.

But I'm not going to talk about the Internet. Not today.

MRS. WILSON

17

Like everybody else I knew, I was intimidated at the idea of moving into Mrs. Wilson's classroom when I entered sixth grade in 1942.

It had always been the mysterious, awe-inspiring Big Room, for grades five through eight, waiting to swallow us up, and Mrs. Wilson was the principal with a reputation.

For a couple of years, they turned the playroom downstairs, into another classroom for 4th and 5th grades, leaving only three grades in each of the two original rooms. After four years with Mrs. Cruise and one with Mrs. Peart, I expected big changes.

Mrs. Wilson, stern, with thin lips and no discernible sense of humor, was older—perhaps even into her forties. She always wore silky print dresses over one of the big heavy corsets customary to older women of the era. It was obvious because they all had the same shape, and many of our mothers wore them. The corset fit over the torso down over the hips, flattening the figure from front to back, forcing the bulk to the sides, effecting a widened, unnatural appearance to the body. I have no idea what the purpose was.

(Except the doctor told Mama to quit wearing those

corsets once when she had a back problem. "What do you need it for," he asked. She told him, "To hold my stockings up." "Quit wearing stockings," he told her. She did, for the most part, and the corsets became a thing of the past for her.)

Mrs. Wilson wore a tight perm, face powder, and sensible shoes with a chunky heel.

In spite of all that, she endeared herself to me the first day. Just after we were seated, she had to leave the room for a few minutes and asked for somebody to write some material on the blackboard while she was gone. I got up and did the job. When she returned she asked, "Who wrote that on the board? That is beautiful handwriting!" Somebody told her who it was, and she seemed pleased.

So at least we started out on good terms. I heard somebody say that people remember mostly the bad things that happen to them and forget the good things. Not me. I like the good things. Of course handwriting, like spelling, is a skill, but requires no particular intellect, so I wasn't out of the woods yet.

Mrs. Wilson, a deeply religious Nazarene who held rigid standards of behavior, had little problem with us because most of us hadn't yet succumbed to any serious vices, and we were fairly well-behaved.

Her demeanor was less threatening than we'd expected, and if you tended to business you were pretty much all right.

When we entered in the mornings, Mrs. Wilson had already written the agenda for the day on the board. So each class knew exactly what the day would hold, and we got started without any further ado from her. Now and then she presented some new material to one or the other of the classes. This took a tremendous amount of organization on her part to keep three or four grades going at once.

Then the various classes moved to a large table at the back of the room to discuss and follow up on different subjects from time to time while the rest of the room went on working on our own. When we finished, we had some options, one of which was to go to the library, a small room off the main classroom; however Mrs. Wilson expected us to go in there to find a book and read, not to get together and fool around. She had a mirror strategically placed so she could see what was going on in there and exact her strict rules.

We had a couple of kids in the room that I always felt sorry for. Bert never seemed able to please the teacher and received scoldings fairly often. He was always quiet, never disruptive nor disobedient, but I'm sure he never heard a kind word from Mrs. Wilson. Maybe he just didn't appear to be working hard enough to suit her. Looking back I think he might have been depressed, but I don't think anybody concerned themselves with that in those days.

We had some new kids come to the area. Leonard was 16 and in the 8th grade, meaning he was 3 years behind in school, and appeared to be fully grown. I think he was bright enough, but he was a smart aleck, husky and well-built and at least a foot taller than the teacher. One day he stood up in a threatening stance and started sassing her. We'd never seen that before! Without hesitation, Mrs. Wilson strode over to him, looked up into his face, and ordered in no uncertain terms, "Sit down and be quiet!" simultaneously putting her hand on his chest and pushing to enforce her order. He fell awkwardly back into his seat, and was silenced. Mrs. Wilson continued on as if mentally brushing her hands of him, doing our hearts good.

Then the McKinneys, Jean and Barbara came. They lived two doors from me, and we got to know them well as good friends. Mrs. Wilson was skeptical from the beginning. They were from California. More worldly than any of us, outgoing, always good-humored and full of fun, using a little saltier language than any of us natives. They might say, "My God, kid!" or "What the heck is that?" Mrs. Wilson was incensed; we didn't swear or use the Lord's name in vain. Once she said, "This used to be a pretty good school until some people came here!" We all, including Jean and Barbara, knew who she meant, and we laughed about it though we didn't let her know it. They weren't in the least intimidated, and continued to feel welcome and accepted.

Mrs. Wilson also did some nice things for us, beyond the call of duty. Once a year she cooked a huge pot of beans and somehow got them into the school building and sitting on the furnace floor register at the front of the room to stay warm until noon when we had our one hot lunch per year. It fed up to 30 hungry kids with as many seconds or thirds as we wanted.

She also threw 4 seasonal parties a year to celebrate our birthdays—for Halloween, Christmas, Valentine's Day and Easter. Each one celebrated the birthdays of those in that quarter of the year, and they got to sit at the back table with a colorful paper cloth and appropriate decor. We all ate heartily, indulged with wonderful and plentiful party foods such as fresh, glazed cake donuts, my favorite, cider and candy corn for Halloween.

We had one field trip a year—literally. An all-day, several mile hike a couple miles down the road and through the fields and hills to bird watch and enjoy the flora and fauna of the season. We carried our lunches, and sat down to eat before returning to school, tired and hot. Mrs. Wilson wore one of her same silky print dresses and I'm quite sure, the same shoes she wore every day, for these hikes. She would never be caught wearing pants. But of course none of the girls did either in those days.

Other customs were music every Friday when we sang from a little yellow song book of "Old Favorites"—folk songs, and Stephen Foster songs. Mrs. Wilson never opened her mouth because she said she couldn't sing, but she loved music, and demanded that we did, so mostly everyone did, with fervor, often favoring her with her favorite song, "When You and I Were Young Maggie."

Before we could leave on Fridays, each in turn, as we filed out, had to recite to her the Memory Gem for the week such as "Make new friends, but keep the old; these are silver; those are gold." That's the only one I've remembered to adulthood. But I got the idea. And I remember the activity fondly. This took some time so we often didn't all get away until about four on Fridays instead of the scheduled 3:30.

One year the state adopted new science books. Mrs. Wilson didn't believe in science or maybe they had something in them about evolution. Whatever it was, she said grimly, and firmly, "I have to give you these, so put them in your desks. You can read them if you want to." That was it for science at Valley View. I took mine out once, and read a little bit. I never saw anyone else reading one.

Mrs. Wilson seemed to enjoy plays, and we learned to too. Twice a year we put on a program for the community with skits, music, and plays. The boys put up the hardwood stage at one end of the room and even rigged up a curtain, which had to be manually pulled for these audience-pleasing performances.

One of the famous ones that was done repeatedly through the years, was a skit called "The Flivver Family." The set was a car made out of whatever old car parts could be found by some of the boys, usually a couple of fenders, a steering wheel, two wheels or tires, and a front and back seat of some sort. It was rigged up in such a way that it could fall apart on cue with a rope tied to an underpinning, and pulled. The boys seemed to enjoy accomplishing that challenging task, of building a car on stage, setting it up fast, and cleaning it out quickly afterwards as well.

A father, mother, son, and daughter were riding in the car when the curtain opened, all of them bouncing up and down, simulating the car driving along on a bumpy road. The mother talked non-stop, with few if any lines from the rest of the family. She prattled on with the latest gossip, frequently interrupting herself to caution her husband about his driving. "Watch out for this curve!" or "Slow down!" or "Be careful; there's another car!" Then she yelled back at the kids, "You kids, straighten up. Behave yourselves!" At the end, something happened. The mother probably yelled, "Watch out for that tree!" after which, the rope was pulled, and the car fell to pieces. All the family fell out. The mother lying immobile on the ground. One of the kids says, "Daddy, daddy, look at mama! What's the matter with her?" Daddy answers, "Her mouth is shut." Curtain.

Strangely, this skit always got a big laugh. A sign of the times I guess.

Once Mrs. Wilson actually showed us she had some carnal knowledge when she included a romantic skit that had a kiss in it. She picked an eighth grade girl for that part who she probably thought had had some experience along those lines so she wouldn't be corrupting anybody.

The kiss was supposed to be a secret and was never practiced. It was done only once—in the actual performance. However we found out about it, and it offered some excitement in anticipation, though I think mostly because it was such a surprise that Mrs. Wilson would allow that at all or that she even knew about such a thing. None of us actually saw it though. We were busy getting ready to go on stage again. Or whatever.

The years in Mrs. Wilson's room were during the war. We participated in metal drives, collecting rubber, and buying stamps for a quarter each, to fill little booklets for the war effort.

Also we raised money to buy a record player for the school and felt quite accomplished and up-to-date with that amenity.

A couple of years after I went on to high school, they

consolidated the elementary schools, and Valley View closed along with the other small country schools, We all felt a great loss. One day, in the music room at the high school, there was our record player, a tribute to Valley View that only we knew about. We all resented that they had closed Valley View and taken our record player. And that nobody knew we had worked, raising the money to pay for it.

Mrs. Wilson turned out to be a good teacher, at least for those of us in her favor. We even found out she did have some sense of humor. Though rarely, sometimes she couldn't help laughing when we did something funny, so she just covered her mouth with her hand. We saw her husband now and then. He was a particularly witty and funny man, and we wondered what they had in common.

She worked hard; we worked hard, but we also had our fun. We had learned to be self-sufficient and self-motivated, and we entered high school ahead in everything except science. We had been taught algebra, and had diagrammed so many sentences that our grammar was honed to a tee, and we delved into Civics. So freshman year in high school was a breeze. Nothing that year was new to us.

We had Mrs. Wilson to thank for that, and for the lifelong memories.

HEY GANG, LET'S PUT ON A SHOW

18

"Pay no attention to what critics say; no statue has ever been put up to a critic." Jean Sibelius

Two of my cousins came to my house one Sunday. Susan was 13 and Freddie, 12, the same age as me. We got to talking about putting on a play. That would be fun. Maybe we could get a bunch more kids to be in it. Shades of Mickey Rooney and Judy Garland!

As we talked about the idea, we got more and more excited. We wondered if Mrs. Wilson would let us put it on at school.

"Maybe we could write one ourselves!" I chimed as I ran for a tablet and pencil. We were on a roll.

Susan and Freddie's demeanor see-sawed as I climbed a ladder of exhilaration. It splashed like a sudden leak into my consciousness that I was the only excited one. They drew back, edged toward the door, and—well—they left.

For about five minutes I was bereft. On a roller coaster of emotions, I'd just been hurtled to the bottom of the ride. But after a few minutes it began to turn into irritation. "What's wrong with them!"

And then determination. "OK, I'll write it myself!"

It had been six years since I wrote anything else of substance. My cousin Bette sent me some letters 75 years later that her mother, Aunt Bessie, had saved. One I wrote when I was six.

> "Dear Susan and Bette,
> How are you? I am fine.
> My turtle got lost.
> I looked for him in the grass.
> Your cousin,
> Jeanette"

So, with that far behind me, I started writing a play.

I wrote and I wrote and I wrote. This was in 1943 in the middle of WWII, of which we were all acutely aware. Our parents carefully spent their ration books on things like coffee, sugar, gasoline, and shoes. Several of us had older siblings away in the war. Some had gold stars in their windows.

So what would be more logical than a play about a family getting ready for Christmas with some of the kids away in the war? That became the essence of the story. I didn't know you needed conflict to make a good story, but it came naturally as the family was sad and forlorn because they had no hope of seeing four of their kids at Christmas. The story contained no villains; the conflict didn't go that far.

One of my main goals was to have a part for every kid in the room. There were 25 or 30 of us so it took some doing to work in that many characters. I have no idea what they all were now, but somehow I did it.

The preacher made a visit to comfort the family. Mrs. Wilson would like that. She was a Nazarene and approved of anything to do with church.

At one point a knock came at the door. It was a man delivering a "singing telegram." I didn't know exactly what that was, so I extrapolated from what I'd heard about them. The play had morphed into somewhat of a musical. Cousin Betty, one of the military kids, and a good singer, would sing the telegram she sent to the family. I would slip in and accompany her on the piano as her husky alto voice floated out "I'll be Home for Christmas," which ends "—if only in my dreams," after which her fanciful being, faded—that is walked—off stage. It was a promise to be home in spirit only. But everyone rejoiced to get her message.

After much lamenting about the absent ones, the play ended on Christmas Eve when, one by one, all the sons and daughters came home when they were given leave at the last minute, for no apparent reason. Much like in a Hallmark production. And a most happy Christmas was had by all.

I didn't know that writers always go back to delete and rewrite. I remember writing just one draft, so that saved me a lot of time and energy.

The next morning I took my finished masterpiece to school and showed it to Mrs. Wilson. "I wonder if we could put it on," I said.

"I'll take it home and read it and see."

The next day, our most strict and demanding teacher, said to me, without my asking, "Yes, you can put on the play. You direct it." (It must have been the part about the preacher.)

"Me?" I hesitated. "Okay. But when can we practice it?"

"We'll work that out. You'll have time to practice. Get your parts all copied for everybody so they can learn them. It's all up to you." Her confidence in me was astounding, and most-likely misplaced, however, while surprised, I don't remember feeling any inadequacy to the task. I was full of enthusiasm. (This was before I lost all my self-confidence.)

That night I spent writing all the parts, by hand, to pass out the next day. (We didn't bother with auditions.) The only copier in our school was the hectograph, an odd setup with a gelatinous surface. With care and special ink, you could make one copy at a time, a long, slow process. Only the teacher used it. So the cast never saw the whole play on paper. I just told them what was happening as we worked our way through until everybody had it learned. We had numerous rehearsals, and somehow it all came together.

We cleared the front third of the room for a stage area, and for the set, had a Christmas tree, the piano at one side of the room, and a few chairs. (That was all right. Even in college when we played a scene from "The Glass Menagerie" at a school in central Oregon, the set consisted of nothing but metal folding chairs. The picture on the wall for "the departed father" was of Harry Truman. It worked.)

All our entrances and exits were through the classroom door on one end of the stage area opposite a row of windows.

111

We made adjustments to the casting based on who was able to come up with some semblance of a military uniform. My brother had left a khaki shirt and cap at home on his leave, so I was a WAC. Somebody else had a sailor hat, and so on. We wound up with a soldier, a sailor, a WAVE, and a WAC.

I hadn't worked out much of an ending except for the family all being together on Christmas Eve, singing carols around the piano before saying goodnight all around and happily exiting to bed at the figurative final curtain, a dimming, that is a turning off, of the lights.

I had delayed asking Mrs. Wilson about my last idea. I didn't expect her to approve. I got my nerve up one more time and asked, "Could Clair," the biggest kid in the room, "be Santa Claus and bring in bags of goodies for the audience at the end?"

"Yes." She agreed.

Then the hair-trigger part. "Could he come in the window?" I thought it would make his arrival more dramatic and surprising than if he just used the same door as the cast. We didn't have a chimney so it was the best I could think of. But it would require him to ascend a two-story ladder at the back of the building and I thought it would be too dangerous for her to allow.

"Yes." She agreed.

Mrs. Wilson provided the bags of goodies, and probably helped Clair get a Santa Claus costume. Somehow she informed the community of the afternoon premiere. We had a full house.

Mrs. Wilson introduced the event. She gave me credit

112

for writing and directing the play, and for including a part for everybody in the room. She said that we had done the whole thing without her help. That wasn't entirely true; she was modest about her contributions. But it is true that she didn't make a single suggestion about the script or the performance. And she denied us nothing that I asked for.

We put on a melodramatic tear-jerker, and there wasn't a dry eye in the house. Well, that's what Bette says. But she's inclined to exaggerate. Maybe some of our mothers welled up. At any rate, it was a hit.

If you doubt that, try to prove it wasn't. The one script that ever existed is forever gone. I never saw it again after that day. We probably put it away in the attic at home. And except for Bette and me, and a few who now live far away, we don't know if any of the cast is still alive. We know that Clair, Dean, two Donalds, Barbara, Doris, Susan, Freddie, and Wilbur are, sadly, all gone. So there's nobody left to ask. You'll have to take my word for it. It could have been a best seller, probably to Hallmark. If it had been marketed.

Afterward—

The "preacher's" mother had a good laugh, since the actor, Jimmy Anderson, had probably never darkened the door of a church, and he was a bit of an imp. But he'd taken his role to heart, took on a certain dignity, and did a great job, standing as tall as possible in his black suit and turned-around collar. I think she was proud of him.

I giggled in embarrassment when somebody introduced me to a real WAC in uniform in the audience. Here I was in this silly get-up. But she tried to put me at ease. "Oh, no, you look fine. And I loved the play." She was the substance of my play in reality—a soldier home for Christmas.

Santa Claus opened and crawled through the window on cue. But I have no idea how. In order to hear the last lines, he would have had to be standing near the top of the ladder for a good bit of that hour-long performance. He stood out there alone in the cold, holding that gigantic bundle of candy, hanging onto a ladder while he waited for his entrance.

Thinking back on it now, I should have had a reprise of "I'll Be Home For Christmas." It would have been a cue for Santa Claus to climb the ladder, saving him some stress. And it would have given a final tug at the heart of our audience. How could I not have thought of that?

I should also have had a curtain call and milked the audience for applause. I don't remember thinking of that. It would have been nice for the cast, and it makes audience members think they liked it even more than they did. The more they clap and watch the actors take their bows, the more they enjoyed the show. But I didn't know about that in those days.

And I really shouldn't have neglected to thank our beloved Mrs. Wilson, our most strict, demanding teacher, who I expected to be my biggest challenge, for softening a little and letting a bunch of kids put on a cornball, melodrama in her venue. For her unmatched encouragement and confidence in us, and for doing so much behind the scenes to make it happen.

I've never directed a play again where I had such complete cooperation. It didn't surprise me then. I just expected it. But looking back, I'm overcome.

All in all, I did it. It felt good to have followed through and completed a task, albeit with lots of help. An exhilarating experience, I learned, though, that you don't do anything alone. You're always indebted to many others, directly and indirectly, a good learning experience for me, early on.

For this one, it took a gang.

SHORTY EDWARDS

19

He was one of those enigmas who was around all of my childhood. And I knew little about him.

What I saw was a quaint little man not much more than five feet tall who wore something akin to a top hat which gave him a little more height. I don't remember ever seeing him without his hat. He was friendly and polite, and seemed happy to be called "Shorty," which was the only name I ever heard for him. I don't remember having any personal interaction with him.

He lived alone in a one-room hut a little way down the road from us. I was never in it, but it was tiny and unpainted. I don't know if it even had electricity or running water, bringing me to wonder how he took a bath and washed his clothes. I never saw a clothesline. But he seemed clean and presentable. I suspected that whoever owned the property just let him live in that little shack. I also guessed that he didn't have a job. He seemed old. But everybody past 30 did in those days. Since my perspective on that score has changed, I realize he was probably in his 40s or 50s at the time.

Shorty was a Seventh Day Adventist. I never thought

about how he got to church every Saturday, 3-plus miles away in town. I never saw him drive a car.

Every Saturday afternoon he knocked on our door as he walked around the countryside, distributing religious tracts. My parents always invited him in, and Mom would say, "Shorty, would you like to eat with us?" He never turned that down. He always answered, "Don't mind if I do." He seemed to enjoy the food and expressed appreciation. We thought maybe he timed his tours so he would arrive at our house just before suppertime. He ate with us many Saturdays, and we heard "Don't mind if I do," every time.

I'm sure there was conversation at the table, but I don't remember what about. It must have consisted of bland pleasantries. I learned nothing of his past or his family. I doubt if he had ever been married or had any woman in his life. My guess is we, and the church were his only social contacts to speak of.

My uncle said that you could knock on Shorty's door at any time in the middle of the night, and he would appear fully dressed with his hat on. I couldn't imagine why anybody would have gone there in the middle of the night. In those days everybody was in bed asleep by 9 or 10, and got up by 6 to start building fires and going to work. So I believed Uncle Cince was just guessing about that and thought it was funny.

However. The family did carol to Shorty one Christmas. We would have arrived some time between 3 AM and dawn on Christmas morning. And shortly he appeared at the window, fully dressed with his hat on. We sang "Song of the Angels" and "Silent Night". He called out his appreciation, lifting his hands toward heaven, "Praise his holy name; I wish I's up there now!" We wondered if our singing had made him wish he was dead.

I learned more, from my brother, many years later, about Shorty. He was a carpenter by trade. Self-employed. He owned his hut, the 40 acres it was on, and raised some livestock. He also owned a Model T Ford for years until he rolled it when its lights went out one night. He said, "That was the darkest black I ever saw." Then he got a Plymouth. He had a brother who came to see him once who was about Shorty's height. Shorty never liked his given name, so didn't tell anybody what it was. My brother said that the only way he could think of to find out was to visit his grave at the Oddfellow's cemetery in Coquille. We haven't done that yet. Maybe we don't even want to.

What I did learn firsthand, is that though Shorty had seemed to me to be of some other time, he was more self-sufficient, up-to-date, and aware than I had thought. During my father's long, bed-ridden illness, just three months before he died, I graduated from the eighth grade. Shorty showed up at our house earlier in the day and offered to stay with my dad that night so Mom could go to my graduation.

Who would have thought that he would have even known I was graduating and when it was happening, let alone that it would have occurred to him that we might need that kind of help? No one else, even of our many relatives in the area, thought of that. Mom couldn't have gone if it hadn't been for Shorty. My mother never forgot him for this kindness, his generosity and thoughtfulness on that night. Shorty Edwards was an odd little man, but he had a beautiful, big heart.

THE GOOD OLD DAYS

20

One of the huge changes from my early days to the present, is the way medical care has been conducted. Though most of the cures and medicines we have today weren't available then, it felt about as close as you could get to socialized medicine where everybody receives the care they need without the complicated systems we have to conquer today in this country.

We had a couple of doctors in Coquille. Our family went to Dr. Richmond. Or more accurately, he came to us. If you were sick enough to go to the hospital, they took you in, no questions asked.

James Richmond was born in Scotland. He came to Michigan in 1908 for his medical training, and then moved to Coquille, Oregon, where he remained for his whole career. He was like a family friend. Some people were critical of him, accusing him of being rough when he treated you and of leaving huge scars from surgeries. That last part was probably true. I never encountered that, and I was never hospitalized. But I know of lives that he saved. Maybe including my own, by performing a simple procedure that I'm not sure everyone would have thought of.

Dr. Richmond took pride in the fact that he never sent bills to his patients. He told about going into the post office to mail one once, and met the recipient coming in as he walked out. He felt so ashamed, he never sent another one. Some speculated that maybe it worked better for him, as he had no record of his income and possibly avoided taxes that may have been assessed. But I prefer not to believe that. I know that some people never paid him.

After he'd done a major surgery for my mother, she asked, "What do I owe you?"

He said, "Just hand me 50 dollars."

She said in astonishment at that conservative request, "Fifty dollars?"

He said in his commonly terse manner, "My dear, if that's too much, just forget it," and walked away. She paid him 50 dollars. And that is all it cost her.

Dr. Richmond lived in a nice but modest house in Coquille. A similar house next to it was the Knife Hospital, everything white, the bedding, the nurses' uniforms, and the walls, inside and out, and always with a strong odor of ether permeating the air. It was owned and run by a nurse, Belle Knife—Aunt Belle to all. She was a jolly, much overweight woman who was also a friend of ours and lived in the lower level of the house with her family, the upper floor used as the hospital. A bridge connected the two houses for convenient access for the doctor. This is where I was born.

The doctor always came out when we called.

I heard a story about when he had to see someone

across the river. It couldn't have been the Coquille River. You couldn't have waded across that. But wherever it was, my mother's brother, Uncle Zed I think, carried Dr. Richmond with his medical bag, piggy back across the stream to see the patient, and back, quite a task, as the doctor was a hefty man, tall and well-filled-out. Imagine that today.

As a toddler I had lots of croup. When I was about four we were at Grandma and Grandpa's place, a quarter mile down the road from us. I was sitting on Grandpa's lap trying to breathe. At some point, I tried to inhale, and it felt like a stone wall had been built in my chest. Zero air. I began to feel panic when the doctor walked in. He immediately stuck his finger in a jar of Vicks Vaporub, one of my mother's standbys, and shoved a big gob of it down my throat. I will never forget that heavenly feeling of fresh air that immediately rushed in. And that did it. It's the only time I was that bad. But I did spend a lot of boring time lying on a quilt on the floor, under a tented sheet with a steamer. My brother told me recently how it "scared him to death" when he saw me turning blue in my croup episodes. I'd never known he cared much about me at all.

We have lots to thank Dr. Richmond for. When my Aunt Bessie was sixteen with a ruptured appendix and gangrene, Dr. Hamilton, who Dr. Richmond had enlisted to assist in surgery, said it was too late and impossible. But Dr. Richmond said, "No, she's too young," and saved her. She lived to 93. Her daughter, my cousin Bette, had a ruptured appendix at nine, and he saved her too by waiting to do her surgery until she was in the rally that sometimes happens just before you die. He believed she could not have survived the surgery until she got to that stage. Then he filled her with sulfa, a new remedy. She's a healthy 81 now. And my life-long best friend.

Another difficult case was a little girl who had been badly burned over much of her body, and the usual painful methods weren't working. Dr. Richmond went to some old medical books, and followed one recommendation of covering the burn completely with adhesive tape, applied directly to the burn, and leaving it there. It was soothing as well as healing, and she recovered with smooth skin. After that my mother always put adhesive tape on her fingers when she burned them, blisters or not, and left it. It worked. I don't know if anybody else knows about the adhesive tape treatment for burns; I've never heard of it from anyone else. But it seems they ought to. It worked beautifully.

It was a whole different world then, and we were lucky to have Dr. Richmond in ours.

Bette thinks he had to have been terribly intelligent. She didn't see him often at all, but she ran into him on the street one day. He came strutting along with his thumbs hooked in his vest, as was his usual style, saw her and said, "Well, hello, my dear, I remember the first time I ever saw you. Sixteen years ago today!" It happened to be her sixteenth birthday. Who would have thought?

A BEST CHRISTMAS

21

Christmases were meager during the depression though I didn't know it. We lived in the country at Coquille with animals and gardens. Food was abundant. I never felt deprived.

Gifts cost a nickel or a dollar. I opened a book, some crayons, or a hankie and felt indulged.

When I was 12, I started talking about a bike. The only one I'd ever had was a man's bike that had been my brother's. It was old, heavy, and rusty. I rode it a lot.

My father was ill and in the midst of two years in bed that he spent before he died. There was no money. That didn't occur to me when I beamed before I went to bed on Christmas Eve, "I'll bet when I wake up there's going to be a new shiny bike sitting right here by my bed."

There wasn't. There were gifts, food, and caroling on Christmas morning.

I realized Mom and Daddy were worried about the bike issue when Mom said that evening, "I'll bet you didn't even think about a bike this morning did you?"

I grew up a little just then when I smiled and lied, "No".

No bike. But a most happy Christmas.

JOHN EDWARD STONE

22

His little brother, five-year-old Neal had just died from typhoid fever, and their 36-year-old mother, Julia Ann, had died a few weeks earlier from the epidemic in 1893. Seven-year-old John survived.

This left their father, David Samuel, John, three older sisters, Nannie, Nettie, and Kitty, and the eldest, a brother Elmer, 13, who "wasn't right" since he had choked on some food when he was younger.

The family had moved to Oregon from Texas in 1886 by covered wagon and settled in an old house up a hollow off Fishtrap Creek near Myrtle Point, Oregon. It was in this house that John was born a few months after they arrived. Later they moved to Milton Freewater in Northern Oregon where the illness and deaths occurred.

Their father never recovered from the losses, and seemed unable to parent his children adequately though he was a loving man, and his children held the utmost respect for him.

They moved back to the Fishtrap area where several relatives of Julia Ann's lived.

At eleven John was hired on a farm where he worked for his room and board, for a man who he disliked because he was mean and often put his wife to bed from beatings he gave her. I don't know how he treated the help.

John finished eighth grade and quit school. It was hard to work full time and go to school too. He later lived with sister Nannie after she got married to Manley Barklow, and part of the time with an aunt and uncle, the Hammacks, and their son Jim who became John's closest friend until Jim died as a young husband and father of two little girls.

John went to Idaho where sister Kitty lived with her husband, Dan Stover, and worked until he got a message from Oregon after the family found out where he was, that they missed him and wanted him back home. He had felt that nobody cared. But he happily returned.

My grandfather, David Samuel Stone, died at age 63 in 1906 when my father John Edward Stone was 20.

My dad became a logger. Loggers are known for being a roughhewn bunch, scarring floors stomping around in their cork boots, and for carousing behavior. But I saw my father as more refined than most of them.

Daddy wore mostly denim overalls held up by suspenders over blue work shirts. Six feet tall, he had a light English complexion but with dark brown eyes and receding jet black hair. He had a trim build, and a loose-jointed walk. Somebody saw me once when I was a teenager, and said he knew I was John's daughter because I walked just like him. He had a black suit, and usually wore a fedora with that. But dressing up didn't happen often after I knew him.

Unfortunately Daddy started smoking when he was 21, his only vice, mostly rolling his own out of a can of Prince Albert from his back pocket. Occasionally he smoked

Camels. He shaved with a straight razor.

He was also a human alarm clock. Daddy could wake us up at any preordained time. He said you just think what time you want to wake up, and you do. When we were going on a trip, we got up at four, on the dot, to get an early start. That was some kind of moral issue with my parents, who never could understand other members of the family who would go places at all hours. Daddy just shook his head in disbelief that anybody could live like that. I learned that rule, but haven't necessarily lived by it during my life, preferring getting enough sleep.

Another thing he couldn't abide was fishing. "I can't think of anything more boring than sitting on a bank waiting for a fish to bite."

He admired gymnastics and I think would have liked me to learn it. He put up some rings for me, hanging from a maple tree behind the house, and talked to me about all the things you could do in that realm. But of course that takes some training, and there was none available that I know of. I also probably didn't have the knack. But I played on the rings some.

Daddy also talked about boxing a lot, and got Boyd a punching bag that they played with occasionally.

As for swimming, that wasn't a choice for me. The only place to swim would have been down the hill in the river where there were a couple of sand bars. Some kids did swim there, but not me. I waded in the edge a few times. But Daddy warned, "Don't ever swim in there. It has a strong undertow." Mama said, "Daddy used to be a strong swimmer, and he pulled a lot of people out of that river.

Some of them he saved." So I didn't learn to swim until I was a senior in high school and went camping with my cousin Glennis and her husband. She taught me the side stroke and convinced me to swim across Pistol River and back, alone, while they watched from the bank. Quite an accomplishment. But swimming never became my forte.

Although he had a difficult childhood and not much formal education, I learned some of the most important life principles from my father including how to live a Christian life. He didn't put it that way, nor did he claim to be a Christian. He just lived like one. "We should always be tolerant," was the way he put it. He was honest in all his dealings, and always generous.

Actually, as for his education, it might be a stretch to call it formal. He told about once when a teacher asked him to spell "punkin." He answered, "P-U-N-K-I-N." "Wrong!"

Kids remember.

My mother was more judgmental than my dad; he generally accepted everybody as long as they weren't criminal and hurtful of other people.

Mom went a little more by whether she liked their looks. That was a common phrase to describe people who appeared to be untrustworthy in some way. "I never did like his looks."

On the other hand, one of her common adages was, when she heard someone being criticized for her behavior, "She's more to be pitied than censured."

I never heard my father say a swear word though he worked and mingled with many who did, and treated them

128

with respect and as friends. In fact he found them pretty funny sometimes.

While he was a loving person, he was suspicious of people who were too demonstrative in their affections. He wasn't. And when he saw married couples who were constantly calling each other pet names, "Honey and Sweetheart", he thought they probably had a marital problem. I don't know if Mom totally agreed with that, but I know she felt secure in him, and I certainly did.

Daddy had many talents. An old wooden lathe stood in our woodshed. As a hobby, he cured myrtle wood, cut it and turned bowls and other decorative objects which he sanded smooth, and varnished to a high shine.

During the depression he made cross bows by hand out of yew wood for a man named Ulrich from Roseburg, who sold them. He spliced them together at the handle and shaped by hand-carving into bows of different strengths, and amazingly they turned out perfectly balanced, just by his eyeballing and sanding them down accordingly. He made me one with a 24-pound pull, his lightest one, as I was probably about eight at the time. We practiced shooting into bales of hay. He won some contests. I wasn't so good at it, and never competed.

Most of the bows were sold in England, bringing in extra income. Daddy always had big hunks of yew wood curing in water for this, and he took pride in the artistry involved in making those bows. In the 1970s after I came back to Eugene, a friend ran across a full page article in the Eugene Register Guard about Ullrich and his bow-making industry of the past. He was still living at that time, probably in his 80s. I should have contacted him.

Daddy also made me a child-sized ironing board which hinged for folding away, just like Mama's, and they gave me an electric toy iron, which got warm.

Daddy invented a couple of things which never got off the ground. One was a monkey wrench, for which he carved a wooden prototype with moving parts, unlike anything available at the time. He planned to obtain a patent, but before he did, somebody else made one that I believe was almost identical to his, which has been a commonly used tool ever since. Everyone has a monkey wrench.

Another of his ideas that I think he and my brother cooked up, which could have been considered a forerunner to some safety features that we have today, such as padded dashes and air bags, was to line cars with all rubber, so that if you had an accident, everybody would just bounce around inside and not get hurt. Well, it gave the rest of us a good laugh anyway.

He also bought into a "gold mine", with a couple of friends, the three of them taking a trip there every year or so. No gold was ever found. I think Mom was a little disgusted with that whole venture.

He and my brother built a row boat in the woodshed, working on it for quite some time, when they started wondering if they would be able to get it out the door or if they would have to tear down the shed. Daddy knew about somebody who had done that, but didn't think about it until theirs was almost finished. Luckily, it came out with an inch to spare.

Daddy worked in the logging industry all this time.

During World War I he made ship's knees out of the root of a tree where it connected to the trunk, making an L shape, and used in building war ships. I had the idea there was one still floating in the South Pacific with Daddy's ship's knees in it. Then I learned that it had sunk near Hawaii in 1937. When he was doing this, he taught himself to file saws that he used for this job, and went on to become a saw filer, which he did during my life time. He was well-known as the "best saw filer in Oregon," and popular with all the buckers and fallers who said they loved using his saws. Once Daddy was fired from a job. I have no idea why. When he left, the whole camp walked out with him. They all got a job together somewhere else.

Saw filing was a more complex job than one would think, requiring a set of different tools, with 6 or 8 steps on each saw. I used to go to work with him one day each summer. The men would all come in and pick up their saws in the morning. It was long and hot. Part of the time I stood and watched Daddy filing. He went through five or six preordained steps on each saw with different tools. I didn't like the harsh, grating sounds, a little like fingernails on a blackboard that I heard on one step. But then some pleasant little clicks, and some slick smooth metallic sounds. I always liked those parts. He had magnets, and I amused myself, moving the fine filings into piles and shapes.

When lunch time finally came around, he came outside and we sat on stumps while we ate, and he fed the little chipmunk who always appeared and climbed up on his knee for a snack. Every year I went, he had a pet chipmunk,

131

who got daily free lunches. Lucky wild animals. Daddy loved animals, and also tamed the chickens at home, feeding them from his hand. He did hunt deer though, and ate fried chicken. It's just that my mother had to kill the chickens as well as cook them. He never would.

At the end of the day, the men would all come back in to leave their used saws to be sharpened the next day, and we made the long drive home after my special day.

Maybe someday we'll get Daddy's saw filing tool set into the Coos County Historical Museum in North Bend. That's where it should be.

I was impressed that my father owned a violin. Of course he was just a fiddler, and played entirely by ear. I heard him only a few times when he played "Turkey in the straw" and such. His cousin and best friend, Jim also had a violin, and I used to picture the two of them running through the hills around Fishtrap with their instruments, which I think they did.

He told about a practical joke he was playing on somebody. He waited inside an old, "haunted" house with a friend, until the victim came by, at which time he would start playing some eerie-sounding music, but before his victim appeared, it back-fired when he heard some eerie-sounding music himself, grabbed the hand of the kid with him, and went tearing out down the mountain. He never knew who pulled that on him.

I remember just one time when Daddy and I had a little misunderstanding. This was during his final illness. One of my specialties on the piano was "Trees." I had played it hundreds of times. But I couldn't improvise a note, couldn't play anything by ear, and had never memorized the piece. I had to read it every time. Everything he played was by ear. One day I was going to play it. Maybe Daddy wanted me to. I'm not sure. But I couldn't find the music. He didn't believe I needed it. I said, "I can't do it without the music." He'd never realized that, and I can see why because I had played it perfectly so many times. He got frustrated, and insisted that I must be able to play it without the music. I got frustrated that I couldn't convince him. I think he thought I was putting on some kind of affectation. But I didn't even know what key it was in. I just looked at the music and played what it said. I always had to memorize note by note, a long procedure, to play anything without music in front of me.

It wasn't serious. We finally dropped it. I found the music, played the song, and everything was back to normal. But I don't know if he ever understood.

On a happier note, during these months, he started talking to me about making plans for when he got well. We would start a myrtle wood business. He stressed that we should use only the burls. Some of them use anything, even the straight grain parts. But the burl is what makes really pretty wood. He would make the items, and I could finish them with the shiny varnish. We spent a lot of time planning this venture. I never told him I didn't really like that shiny finish which was commonly done on myrtle wood objects. There was a lot of that around Coos County, the center of myrtle tree country. And it was widely advertised that myrtle trees grew only in Coos County and the Holy Land. I prefer to believe that whether it's true or not though it probably isn't. Years later, some myrtle wood dealers started using a matte finish, possibly oil, and I liked it much better. But it didn't matter. We had a good time making plans.

Daddy died in 1945 when he was 59, and I was 14.

I always thought, and still think my father was an exceptional person who could have done almost anything with the right opportunity. I think he was bright and talented with an artistic nature. He just never had a chance. But he contributed a lot with what he had, and my life has been richer for it.

23

My mother was one of those special people who lived in three centuries. She rode in a covered wagon from Arkansas to Texas and in a jet plane from Oregon to Germany and back. She never had much but wanted for nothing. Always satisfied, she never complained and stated frequently that she was contented with her life and what she had.

She loved flowers, especially pansies because of their faces, but, as she said with a flair for the dramatic, her favorite flower was "the one I'm looking at."

She hated to cook, but did it faithfully though much preferring cleaning up afterwards, washing dishes, clothes, and most anything. She was the epitome of "Cleanliness is next to godliness" and considered good housekeeping one of the highest virtues to be attained. She approached it, as she did everything, methodically and relaxed, her only related stress seeming to come from not being able to instill the same qualities in her children.

Mom went to school through only one year of high school. This was due to her being kept home so much to take care of her mother when she was "sick".

Grandma tended to use her health to control situations. And was somewhat of a drama queen. Like going to bed sick every time one of her kids was contemplating marriage. When my mother's youngest sister Verna was going to marry Darrell Cox, Grandma said, "Don't do it! Look at what a mess Minnie and Bessie made," referring to my mother and Aunt Bessie and their marriages. My dad found that most amusing. He was a good provider, husband, and father, and widely admired by others. Grandma liked him too. He even supplemented their meager income every month for years. She just said whatever she could think of to get her way.

In high school literature we read a short story called, "The Eldest". The author must have known my mother. It told about a girl who was always held responsible at home because she was the eldest girl.

Mom had to make all the beds and wash the dishes every morning before she went to school. I'm not sure why the siblings couldn't have made their own beds. She had four brothers and two younger sisters. Aunt Bessie and Aunt Verna went on to Normal School and became teachers. Mom finally gave up and didn't return for her sophomore year because it was just too much pressure for a conscientious student. For her last year in school, she lived in town with another family and worked for her room and board. Then went home and worked on the weekends. She had what they called a "nervous breakdown".

She told me she had sworn she would never make one of her children do all the work that Grandma made her do as a child. When she was too small to reach the sink without kneeling on a chair, she did the dishes every day for a family of seven kids, and she often came home from school to piles of dirty dishes created when her mother had quilting bees and fed lunch to the guests. Grandma loved cooking more than cleaning up.

I'm sure that is why I was never expected to do much of anything until I was about 14, and she decided I should help on Saturdays before I took off to town to see a show with friends. I think she got tired of doing everything by herself. Justifiably. It took a little adjustment for me. But not long. And I got some satisfaction from it. It had just never been part of my routine beyond washing or drying dishes sometimes, or dusting the piano keys, and other odd jobs. Once in a while I decided on my own to wax the living room floor and polish it. But that was never done otherwise. Floor waxing wasn't in our repertoire, so it didn't relieve Mom of any work. I just did that for fun.

Sometimes the first thing I heard in the morning was a click, click, click as Mom connected up the hooks and eyes of her girdle, straightened the seams of her silk stockings— no nylon in those days—put a homemade apron on over her print house dress, and went to work, cleaning, cooking, washing, sewing, gardening. She never stopped. Her unusually pretty hands were always rough and scratchy, especially noticeable when rubbing Vicks on chests.

For as long as I can remember, Mom and I went to Grandma's house every Saturday and spent the day cleaning. Mom did her washing, hung it out, brought home the ironing, and took it back down to her when it was done a day or two later. I helped some, mostly with the black dust cloth that always waited for me on the end of one of the stairs, which I walked around the house with and

137

rubbed over the furniture, the colonnades, the piano, and window sills.

In spite of her formal education being cut short, Mom had done well in school apparently, judging by a workbook or two that I've seen in later years. She wrote a beautiful hand and beautiful letters. She didn't read a lot until later years when she had time. Other than that, she had a Bible beside her bed, and always read it for a while before sleep.

My mother had dreams. She always wanted to be a nurse—an RN, and to see Australia. Maybe it was the kangaroos. That wasn't to be.

But she did start nursing after my father died. He didn't believe in insurance so we had no income except $33 a month for me from the recently enacted Social Security program. Boyd had sent home part of his meager income from his military service during the whole time he was in. They weren't paid much, and I don't know how he got along without all of it.

While she had no training, Mom was a kind, caring, and hard-working practical nurse, and was credited for that by her employers. A couple of young RNs said they learned more from her about nursing than from any other source.

During those early years, starting in 1945, she worked for the small Knife Hospital in Coquille, and she was usually alone on the night shift with its 10 to 20 patients. She gave medications, and many complimented her for her painless shots. Those were the days when all the patients in the hospital got a back rub every night. She was a strong proponent of that. Through the years she became an LPN on the job.

I admit, Mom went overboard a little. She was a bit judgmental and critical of some who weren't as good at keeping a clean house as she was. There was nothing worse than having a spider web in your house. In contrast, I've been known to leave a big one in a window on purpose for a Halloween decoration. He seemed to know what he was there for, staying right in the center of his web. But I don't think Mom was around at the time.

A devout Christian, my mother also entertained an element of irreverence. Something about the solemnity of a church service brought on her ability to see the humor in almost everything. The resulting uncontrollable laughter (that she passed on to me and my daughter Christy) caused me to decline to sit with her in church in later years for fear of being caught up in the infectious giggling that seemed to get worse with time. We always tried to suppress it, but the minister noticed and said on one of these occasions, "This is serious business folks," which didn't help. Fortunately Mom's sense of humor extended beyond church services. So we had lots of times when we could laugh as loud and long as we wanted.

Mom often said, "I feel so sorry for the human race." Brought up in the Southern tradition of racial prejudice, she rose above this through the years—or maybe she never harbored it at all. She thought it was terrible that any people were mistreated at the hands of others or were looked down on in this way. Her favorite scripture, Matthew 25:35, the heart of Christianity, ends with "Verily I say unto you, Inasmuch as you have done it unto one of the least of these, my brethren, ye have done it unto me."

Maybe her role in life was defined by her mother who used to say of her three daughters, Bessie's my smart one, Verna's my pretty one, and Minnie's my good one.

Mom liked dolls, fried chicken and potato salad, lemon meringue pie, milkshakes, and no matter what, could put away a big slab of rhubarb pie— à la mode. In spite of which, she stayed pretty trim throughout her life. Holland, her morning coffee, the color yellow, home, and Christmas were all at the top of her list of likes, but Don Knotts and W.C. Fields were not far behind. I remember when she was with us in Washington, D C, hearing her and her son-in-law Mel (that would be my husband) sitting up 'til all hours, laughing at W. C. Fields movies.

She liked babies and birds, but didn't particularly favor cats that often killed the birds. When reminded that that comes naturally to cats, she replied, "Yes, and it's natural for me to kill a cat too." But this was just talk; she was never known to harm a cat. And we had several through the years.

One thing she didn't like was tea. Her sister Bess insisted she drink some after a surgery one time, and she could never tolerate it again. As close as they were, she would still tell, 50 years later, about how she used to like tea 'til Bess ruined it for her. And Bess would nearly always tuck in a tea bag with Mom's presents on gift-giving occasions.

Mom took care of my dad for his last two years when he was bedridden. When he died she was 48. Her son was overseas. The war had just ended. Her father died one month later, and she took in her mother who lived with her for another 15 years, basically tying her down between that and the nursing job. She still managed to get me through college. And she never complained. "This is the day which the Lord hath made; rejoice and be glad in it," was one of her favorite sayings.

Mom did get to see a lot of Europe. She flew alone, her first airplane ride, at age 66, to Germany to visit us for several months, meeting the test of O'Hare Airport. We took trips to Holland, around Germany, and travelled through Austria, Switzerland, Italy, and France with Mel's parents who came over for a short stay too. She saw many sights and we went to a public audience with Pope Paul VI, where we saw him up close.

When we returned to the US in December of 1963, Mom met us in Washington, we celebrated Christmas in a shabby motel, and stayed for several more months before returning home and back to work for another seven years. She got to see many of the high spots— Ford's Theatre, the White House, the Capitol, Supreme Court, the Smithsonian, and Arlington Cemetery with the Kennedy flame.

I'm glad she did get to see a good piece of the world. And I think she fully enjoyed it. She even dressed up in Dutch garb for a picture in Amsterdam.

At 73, she came to San Antonio to be with us, and didn't go back to work at home after that. When I broke my wrist though, back in Eugene, and couldn't do a thing, she came to Eugene to stay with us, and did all the work that got done. She was 92. She went up and down stairs as necessary, cooked, cleaned, went to the basement and washed clothes, and carried them up two flights. I think my

141

house was in better shape than usual during that time.

Mom was always there for us. She loved her grandchildren. Christy could always get her laughing. She was encouraging to all of them in their endeavors—their music, Todd's paintings, and Christy's interior decorating. At one of Littlejohn's concerts, her favorite piece was one with a lively rock beat. And she appreciated my brother's four— Sharon's nursing ability and spirited personality, Marilyn's artistic ability, Johnny's mechanical skills, and Terry's all around sweetness and vast talents. They grew up next door to her, so they were all close. She visited us from time to time, and stayed with us for her last year. She especially appreciated Scott who was so caring and did everything for her during a period when she was sick and staying with us.

She did have two surgeries in her life, and a few illnesses. But she never had high blood pressure, varicose veins, swelling of the ankles, or any of the chronic conditions that cause ill health or require medication. The only medicine she used at the end was eye drops for glaucoma.

We had introduced her to garage sales since we'd come back to Oregon, and she got addicted to those. I think it was a frivolity that she hadn't had much of in her life. To the extent that I was about worn out from it one day. "Are there any more?" she'd ask after we'd been to six or eight. I'd find another one. We had a good time, but I could last only so long.

In her Grandparent's book, she gave her grandchildren the following advice: "Observe the Golden Rule. Be honest in all your dealings. Set your goal high and strive to reach it. Love your enemies. Keep looking up and smile and the world will smile with you. Don't talk too much. I tried that, and it doesn't pay. The tongue is an unruly member and causes lots of trouble and heartaches." To the question, "Have you ever been very wealthy?" she replied, "Yes, I'm very wealthy now. Don't get me wrong. Not as the world calls wealth. I am one of the richest ladies in the land. My cup runneth over."

Don't get me wrong either. My mother didn't speak all the time in lofty Biblical style. She was very down to earth. She just used these quotes from time to time as interjections to life. It was more typical of her to hark back to some guy she'd known who said "My brother's igner'nter'n hell." Or imitate another old man who used to say, "I'm gonna go work in the barn; that's what I'm gonna go work in." So Mom would say in early spring, "I just want to tear up the earth!" Then, "I'm gonna go out and tear up the earth; that's what I'm gonna go out and tear up." And she'd go out and work in her flowers.

Things were pretty slow for her in the last couple of years. She couldn't do much, couldn't see nor hear well enough for TV or to read, and missed out on conversation. But she still got up and dressed every morning. She had said for years that that was important, that you need to keep moving. She died in 2000 at age 102, just 6 weeks short of 103, having outlived all of her many old friends, and every member of her family by a decade.

I wish I could say that we filled in the gaps for her during those last years. But I know we didn't.

Mom left the following poem for her grandchildren—I think it was from memory:

"I shall not care what blunders you may make,
What petty losses you may bid me share.
I shall not fret about each small mistake.
Stay clean and manly and I shall not care.
Shun all that's shameful. That is all I ask.
When you depart let men be glad you came.
Give all you can of courage to your task.
Then if you fail, have failure free from shame.
I would not bind you with parental chains, nor
have you think to please me your must win.
Fail if you must, and still my love remains.
I only ask you not to stoop to sin.
Use what you have of judgment and of tact.
With all men, keep your dealings true.
Beware not blundering, but the shameful act.
Further than this, I would not counsel you."

Edgar Guest

24

"Oh, yes," she said, "He always comes around all dressed up in his suit and tie, looking all important."

That was Mama, and it was derogatory, about anybody who fit that description. The general consensus was that men who went around in suits and ties were just putting on airs unless they were going to church, a wedding, or a funeral. Yet there were exceptions.

The preacher was expected to dress that way. It was appropriate for him. He wasn't a working man, and he had status. Whether he was well-educated or had just picked up on it, and learned to "preach". (And we had some who had evidently come up that way.) It was proper for him to dress according to his station. It would have seemed odd to see him in anything more casual. And there seemed to be others who we accepted. I think maybe it depended on who we liked. I know Mama was fond of many of the business men in town who dressed up every day. And professionals, doctors and lawyers mostly escaped her scrutiny.

But those who rose to the title of "working men" were those who wore overalls and blue work shirts and did hard physical labor. Those were the only ones who were honored with that designation. Most men with desk jobs weren't considered working men. "Never worked a day in his life. Just sits at a desk all day."

If Daddy felt the same way, he wasn't as vocal about it. I'm not sure. He had a black suit, but the occasions for him to wear it were rare after I knew him. Well, the funerals. We had a lot of those.

But he was more accepting of people in general. Boyd probably went along with Mama. I felt a little more like an outsider on the whole subject. I don't remember ever sharing that opinion. I just knew that was the way some people saw it.

And then there was Uncle Doc.

He wasn't anybody's uncle that I know of. We just called him that. Everybody except Daddy, who called him Doc. He was a little, old man with a rim of white hair and a white mustache who stood straight and dignified, and we never saw him in anything but a black suit, white shirt, and tie. The only place I saw him was when he came to visit us every year for two weeks. There was nothing negative about Uncle Doc that I know of. We all loved him and welcomed him wholeheartedly, even in his suit and tie. We talked about how he dressed and chuckled a little. But that was just him, even when he was down in the country with us in our humble abode with no inside bathroom facilities. Even when we took him to the beach, or were out and about the place. I think we found it quaint and endearing in him.

I don't know where he slept at our place. I think he started coming even before we had put in the living room between the kitchen and the bedroom. We must have just squeezed a cot for him into the kitchen someplace though I never saw an extra cot around either. I don't know where we would kept it. There's no explanation for some things. I never saw him in a bathrobe. He was always up and ready for the day when I saw him, looking fresh and happy to greet the day.

Uncle Doc had been married to a cousin of Daddy's who I'd never known, and by then was living with his daughter Franklin, who he called "Frankie," in her big stately house up in the west hills of Portland. At his birth his parents had named him Doctor, maybe hoping he would grow up to become one.

I don't know much about his background, but I think he'd done a variety of jobs growing up. I felt he was well-educated, and I knew he'd been an editor of the Coquille Valley Sentinel for a time. All I really remember about him was how likeable he was, that he liked to come to our place, and we always kind of wondered why. He like to work cross word puzzles, and his eyes commonly welled up, even when he laughed sometimes. I believe he was deeply sentimental about some things. My brother has told me how he was good at manual tasks such as helping him work on a vehicle where they were constructing some kind of trailer that required hammering a nail straight enough to go through two holes. He did one and it met the second hole perfectly. Boyd thought it was a lucky shot. But then he went around to the other side and did the same thing without hesitation. And he swung one of those huge scythes to cut tall grass on our place after Daddy was gone. He did that expertly. All dressed up in his suit.

As I grew up the working class bias always stayed with us even though it was kind of a dichotomy. Because I also heard admiration for highly educated people that we liked. "Oh, yes, he's an intelligent man. He went to college. And he used to be a businessman!" Or "He was a school teacher."

Mom was glad for me to get a higher education. She never pushed me to, but she made great sacrifices to help me do it, and she certainly approved. I know she'd always preferred to have had one herself.

I think I harbored an opposite attitude about admiring the "working man" early on because I have realized an increasing admiration throughout my life, for people who do some of the work that I used to consider menial. I now recognize that all jobs take skills and talents and abilities, most of which I don't have, and I highly admire in others. I've done menial work, like cleaning, working in the laundry and the plywood mill. But some I could never learn. Greasy mechanics are way beyond me. I could never learn how to fix anything. I who usually can't even figure out how to open a spice bottle or use an automatic can opener without help. Or people who build houses. I could never master the precision that requires.

I do recognize in myself a tendency to not see over self-confidence in people as an admirable trait. My husband and I discussed that, and he agreed. You see people who tend to take over in all situations and run things when they are clearly not equipped for the job. There was a General at Fort Sam Houston who rewrote some of Mel's writing, making it unintelligible. He was probably just trying to demonstrate his superiority. Mel was an excellent writer, and that was frustrating for him.

When I transferred to another school once, the principal did that to me too. She rewrote the first paragraph of my bio that she had asked for, to be shared with the other teachers. She made it ungrammatical and made me look like a fool in a new school. She did it on purpose. The general probably just thought he knew best.

For other examples of people in positions beyond their capacity, you need go no further than to look at some of the members of Congress.

While I remained neutral about some of the sentiments, I think I learned the lesson that pride of self is not something to be proud of. And I recognize in myself some effort to avoid taking on any appearance of that trait, even at the risk of burdening my friends with the discomfort of feeling they need to reassure me. I apologize for that. But I've learned my lesson. (Some people have pointed out that I have a tendency to always apologize) so I apologize for apologizing.

But I want it known that my modesty is genuine. No putting on airs for me.

JOHNNY MARTIN'S HOUSE

25

We always did a lot of laughing in our family, sometimes hysterically when we just couldn't stop. A definition of humor is elusive, it is so often different from one person to another.

Some people laugh at jokes, but my family didn't. We would just stare blankly when we heard one. My husband's family would use puns or tell jokes and laugh, but they never laughed out of control as we did. I thought they laughed more just to be pleasant and to show appreciation for the wit or cleverness. I can appreciate that too, if I get the joke, but I rarely find one funny. Because I usually don't get them.

We laughed at people, their and our foibles. Not exactly what you would call high comedy.

I used to do a lot of entertaining, always playing the comedic parts in plays, singing funny songs, and getting lots of laughs. I told my husband Mel once, "I've gotten a laugh when I didn't even get the joke." He said, "I'm not surprised."

My father used to tell funny stories, mostly on himself.

Once in the 1920's he stopped by a shop where they were making road signs, as there began to be more cars on the roads, and a concern about safety on the roads became an issue. Some of them were speeding around at 26 miles an hour. A man in the shop was painting signs that said, "SLOW UP". My dad said, "It seems like it would be better to say 'Slow down' instead of 'Slow up'. I don't know whether the guy changed his wording or not, but Daddy said it was years later before he realized that it was a moot point, and just "SLOW" would have done the job.

On a drive to Eugene from the coast in 2013, I saw two handmade signs that said, "Slow Up!" A reminder of that story. Some people haven't learned any more than they knew in the 1920's, or they have a good sense of humor.

Another story Daddy told was about when he was riding a bike along a country road where there were lots of Himalaya blackberries, growing as they do in much of Oregon since somebody brought them from England and sold them all over the country. They are aggressive plants, producing 20-foot extremely thorny vines in one season. He was looking down into a tangled mass of these briars at the side of the road and thought how awful it would be if you rode off into that, at which time he rode right off into it and found out. "Oooh, it was awful," he said, shaking his head in disbelief. "Don't think too hard about things, because you'll make yourself do something you don't want to do," he told us.

Then we had a running gag in the family that I heard for years before I knew what it was about. There was a house in Coquille on a main drag in that little town of about 4,000, so we often drove past it. Every time, Mom always said, "There's where Johnny Martin lives," and chuckle.

There was nothing innately funny about that. It meant nothing to me.

Years later she explained that when Daddy was working in a logging camp, another logger rode to work with him every day. Every time they passed that house the guy would say, "There's where Johnny Martin lives." It was driving Daddy crazy. "Every time!" he said. He was about to put the guy out and let him walk. My generally calm, good-natured father had been driven almost to the brink. So from then on Mom would always say, "There's where Johnny Martin Lives" every time we passed the house.

I don't know which was the funniest, the fact that the guy always said it, my dad's frustration with hearing it twice a day, or Mom repeating it for him, filling in where his rider left off. When Mom said it, he didn't give her much of a reaction. Just tolerated it I guess.

We never quit saying it. The house is long gone now, but every time I pass that spot, I still say, "There's where Johnny Martin lives." I don't think any of us ever knew who Johnny Martin was.

We didn't have to be in church or some other serious event to start laughing uncontrollably, but it often happened, mostly by my mother and me, some female cousins, and my daughter Christy. We didn't actually laugh out loud, but only with the utmost deliberate effort to suppress it. It was agonizing. It wasn't because we weren't devout, to some extent or another, but just because things were so funny, and if one of us would start, the others were sunk. I think my mother was mostly the cause of it. To the point that I quit sitting with her in church after some years of that misery.

Once she and I were sitting by my grandmother, Mom's mother, when she was about 90, in the Emmanuel Baptist Church. Grandma was audibly shuffling through her Bible looking for the Scripture Reading so she could follow along as we were admonished to do.

When the preacher was almost at the end of the reading, she gave up and said in disgust, "Oh, pshaw, I can't find it" out loud. And clunked the book shut. Mom found that funny, and it spread to me. So the two of us fought laughing out loud for the rest of the long service. I'm not sure if it was Grandma or Mom that was the funniest to me, but laughter is definitely contagious.

Then one time Mom and I were sitting together waiting for church to start when she said, innocently, "I wonder if we're having a choir today." Sometimes we didn't in that small church with an attendance of 40 or 50 because there weren't always enough choir members there to constitute a quorum. I answered, innocently, "I don't know. There's Mrs. Fish sitting over there."

That struck Mom funny, I suppose because Mrs. Fish was never known to sing in the choir, and we didn't actually know if she could carry a tune. I don't know why I said it. But we sat there trying unsuccessfully to get our minds off it. We might take a deep breath and sit still for a few seconds, and then one of us would start jiggling, which got the other one going again.

Usually when we left church, we would start blaming each other. My mother, my daughter, and my cousin Bette, tend to blame me. Bette has actually accused me of doing it on purpose. Well, it's true I have been known to reach over and touch one of them on the leg, or move my foot over to nudge a foot, when I heard or saw something I thought they might appreciate. I couldn't resist. But Christy has done that to me too, so at least she can't blame me for everything.

Christy and I would take Mom to church when we visited her in later years. One time Mrs. Bruce was preparing to perform the Special Music. Her husband at the back of the church was trying to work the recorded accompaniment, sort of a gospel karaoke, and it kept starting in the middle of the introduction so she made several false starts before she raised her voice in exasperation to tell him so he would hear her, "Start at the beginning!" He finally got it, and she sang the song. She didn't have much of a voice anyway, rather shrill, and it was a very dramatic piece. Mom started it, by saying, on her last shriek at her husband, "Oh, my stars." So all in all it was too much for Christy, and I joined in against my will. Here we were out-of-town guests. In my old church. Christy feigned a cough a couple of times to hide a guffaw, which didn't help.

We really didn't openly laugh at anybody; in fact we tried to suppress our giggling because we didn't want to embarrass ourselves or make anybody feel laughed at.

But in the church choir one Sunday, Bill Knight, an older man who sang bass, somehow got behind in the special number, with several words to go when the song ended. He went ahead and finished anyhow after the rest of us were through, and then said, "Well, I made 'er". The whole congregation laughed that time.

One event I wasn't present for, but just the telling of it was enough. Mom told me the story.

Early on a Sunday morning, Aunt Eunice came by Mom's house to drop off a tall vase of glads for her to take to church that morning to decorate.

Mom's hair was still in pin curls with some kind of plastic hair dryer on her head that I'm told blew up some way like a big blue balloon. She came to the door and said, "Oh, how pretty," taking the flowers, "I'll just set them over here on the coffee table," as she started into the other room, proceeding to trip on a chair leg as she went by, which sent her careening back and forth trying to catch herself for the full length of the living room, finally falling flat on the floor with the big vase of flowers landing upright on the coffee table, "just where I wanted them, without spilling a drop of water," she said. Fortunately she wasn't hurt either.

Aunt Eunice just stood helplessly at the door laughing 'til she was weak. She said, "I couldn't have done a thing if Minnie had broken every bone in her body."

There was one joke that we all laughed at. When Mom visited us in Germany, in 1963, we took her to the Officer's and Civilian's club to see Morey Amsterdam, the comedian, who was performing. He was a little short guy with a quick delivery that could make anything funny. He said, "Did you hear the one about the bald-headed shoe salesman and the near-sighted fat woman? He was leaning down trying shoes on her when she looked down and saw

155

his head, thought it was her knee, and put her dress over it." Mom laughed all the way home and the next day. We all did, and it's the only joke I've remembered that that bore retelling in all these years.

I wonder if all of this laughing had anything to do with the fact that Mom lived to almost 103. I kind of think so.

26

Aye, therein lies the mystery. There are certain clues. But few. It is a mystery that will never be solved, (So don't hold your breath) but one fascinating enough to keep the next generation guessing, well three of us anyway.

The three sisters, Minnie, Bess, and Verna are at the heart of it. Minnie, the eldest, born in 1897, Bess in 1903, and Verna in 1906, were the daughters of Edwin Benjamin and Genarah Catherine Finley, who also had four sons, Guy, Elihu (Hugh), Cincinnatus (Cince), and Zed.

It became a mystery only after it was too late to ask any of the principles. Only a few of the 20 cousins in the next generation remain. My brother, 90, is the oldest, and he doesn't know. Most of the rest of us are far afield now, leaving only cousin Bette, Aunt Bessie's daughter, and Virginia, Aunt Verna's, to consult.

Our solution is just speculation, based on the clues—sparse, but clues nevertheless.

Bette, Virginia, and I have faint memories of a name at the core of this mystery, memories which would have never been aroused, had it not been for the scarf.

We guess there has never been more than one person with this first name. When you hear it you'll know why. And it was likely the name of a young man. That is because when one of the sisters would say it, the others giggled.

Only Bess or Verna brought it up, and I heard it only in Minnie's presence. It seemed to be directed at her. They chuckled, and Minnie might have given a wry smile, or even laughed along with them. Nothing more needed to be said. It was all in good humor. Was it teasing? Was it a joke?

I am sure my mother would have let me in on the secret, but it didn't occur to me to ask, and it didn't occur to me that at some point it would be too late and I would wonder. She had told me about a boyfriend, Lloyd Irvin, who, she said kind of wistfully even though she was happily married to Daddy at the time, that "He came very close to being your father." His picture showed a tall, slim, good-looking blond boy. But he died at about age 20 from tuberculosis. There was never any such allusion to this other person.

My mother owned a number of dresser scarves. I was familiar with the one with the pink edging all around and the pink crocheting at both ends. I probably ironed it a few times through the years. I mostly ironed the flat things when I was learning that skill. When she was "through with them," I brought home a stack of lovingly-made linens, doilies, hankies, and dresser scarves, giving no particular thought to the pink-edged one.

Until a few years later when I looked through and inspected the fine work on these remnants from my past.

That's when I saw it. The cloth is of delicate white cotton, four feet long, adorned with three inches of intricate crocheting at each end, and five inches of fringe hanging from it. "Somebody went to a lot of work," I thought, musing from my current perspective and as somebody who never learned to crochet. It was well-used with a quarter inch frayed spot in the middle, and the fringe looks faded and scraggly now.

By looking closely and intensely at this work of art, I detected letters. "M-I-N-N-I-E" was crocheted across the end. My mother's name. I looked at the other end. Sure enough, another name. It took a minute. "F—L—O—U—R-NOY". What? Who could have made this? And why? It came seeping back into my brain. That's the name! Flournoy! I felt like Helen Keller at the water pump when it all came together for her.

I had to tell Bette. And then I called Virginia. Putting two and two together, we surmise, and agree that Aunt Verna was the one. She did the fanciest crocheting and would do anything for a laugh. This was during the hope chest years. If any of the sisters had one though, it was probably an apple box or an orange crate. They were not a well-to-do family, Grandpa being a dirt farmer to support them.

Could this have been for Mom's hope chest? It must have been a tease. Had there been a flirtation? Was Flournoy sweet on Mama? If he'd been a serious suitor I'm sure I would have known.

In September, 2013, Bette told me, in one of our lengthy phone calls, about a stack of old family pictures she went through. One was an unidentified picture of a dorky-looking young man wearing a suit with too short sleeves and legs. She thinks it's Flournoy! "It must be. Who else could it be?"

That's it. That's all we know, and all we can surmise. A name, the way we heard it, and a dresser scarf that pairs the name with my mother's. I can't wait to get a copy of the picture that might be of Flournoy, to go with the mysterious dresser scarf. And I will include this story so that any progeny who might care, will have as close to an answer to this mystery as there will ever be.

The question still hovers. Who was Flournoy, and what was he to my mother? And who would name a baby Flournoy? Although I did learn that it is French, meaning either "one who lives among flowers" or a "free man".

Did my mother have a past that we'll never know about?

If miraculously any other clues to a solution ever arise, I promise there will be a sequel.

But for now, all I can do is hope that poor Flournoy found somebody who gave him the respect he deserved and that he lived among flowers.

HIGH SCHOOL, THE DREAM AND THE FACT

27

By the time I neared eighth grade at Valley View School, I still thought Hollywood shows pictured the real world.

I'd pretended to be Shirley Temple for several years, and by the time I was 10 began to morph into Gloria Jean, the beauty of the teenage hits I saw at the Liberty Theater. She had a head full of curls and a coloratura voice.

After graduation from Valley View, I looked forward to high school and the beginning of moving out into the real world.

I expected Donald O'Conner to be dancing down the halls, bouncing off the walls, and I would be Gloria Jean, singing "You and the Night and the Music" with an orchestral accompaniment wafting in from somewhere while all the kids stood around entranced and in awe.

Actually I was more like Peggy Ryan, their awkward sidekick, and my voice was a little lower. I usually sang alto.

The graduates at Valley View that year included six boys and two girls, both named Jeanette. Myself of course, and Jeanette Epps who lived up in the hills at the end of Glen Aiken Road. I'd never been that far up. She and her brother Vernon cut across the hill through the woods to get to and from school. I just walked a half mile down paved

Highway 42 to home.

She was a nice, quiet girl, but I never got to know her outside of school.

The Epps' were Seventh Day Adventists so Jeanette didn't go on to high school with us, but went to an Adventist Academy instead. So it was Freddie, Clair, Dean, Don, Virgil, Wilbur, and I who went on to high school together.

Guess what I did in the halls of Coquille High School during breaks between classes and after lunch.

For the first few weeks, I stood around by myself, wondering where Donald O'Conner was, watching everybody else laughing and talking in groups, and trying to figure out how to fit in.

I finally decided to just act. Two freshman girls seemed to always be together. I knew them from church, but we'd never been close friends. Kathleen Brockman and Mary May Miller. I don't know what I said to them. Probably, "Can I hang around with you guys?"

Whatever I said to them, they showed no hesitation in taking me in. From then on we became a trio—for the rest of high school. My dad had just died on the first day of school so I wasn't on top of the world anyway. It helped a lot to make some friends. I've always felt grateful to Kathleen and Mary May from then on.

We didn't have much in common. I was serious about school, and they didn't appear to be. But they knew how to act silly and giggle incessantly. I had also taken on the role of a clown so we matched on that score. And we had a lot of fun together.

Everybody got to know me eventually because I did a lot of entertaining at assemblies, and I was in all the plays, in the comedy parts. I was even voted the "wittiest" as a senior. However that was a misnomer for me. They mistook silliness and comedy for wit.

Though I remained in that trio, my circle of friends widened to include new kids to school who we always befriended, and to kids in other grades as well.

One month after school had started, the English teacher came to me during class and said there was a message that Freddie and I were to go right home after school that day. I knew. Grandpa had been sick for a while. It was just a month after Daddy that Grandpa died.

I never did see Donald O'Conner or Gloria Jean. I realized that I'd been on a pipe dream based on the movies.

But I still believed that most of the housewives in the outer world, which I hadn't seen yet, went around the house all day in high heels and fancy coiffed hair.

And I knew they spent all their evenings in formal dress out dancing in nightclubs.

MY GLEN PLAID SKIRT

28

It was the year of The New Look. 1948. I was a senior in high school, and I learned more that year than what was in the curriculum.

The look was long, slim-cut skirts that stopped just short of the ankle. All the style-setters wore them. At least at Coquille High School. Typically a simple short-sleeved pullover sweater above it, bobby sox rolled down as far as possible to the saddles below, and a string of pearls completed the outfit. Glen plaid was the fabric of choice, and I began to want one—bad. My mother sprung $15, an exorbitant amount for us and for a garment of any kind. I already had two of the sweaters, but of a more economical sort.

I wore that skirt almost every day for the whole year, alternating the sweaters from day to day. Nothing else seemed to do. Mine was in subtle shades of grays and blues so maybe nobody noticed that I wore the same skirt daily.

Some people began to take a different attitude toward me. Or maybe I just imagined it because I felt so stylish in my new skirt.

The office recruited some senior girls each year to spend their study hall periods as an office assistant. It was a job to be aspired to. I was one. The job mainly entailed delivering messages to classrooms. We had no loudspeaker system in the school. It made you feel pretty important as everybody looked up when you walked in, and of course I was always in the skirt.

It didn't seem to matter that this "style" was not becoming to me; that wasn't a concern of mine. It was in!

Everybody had always been friendly to me, but we understood the caste system. Our large group of friends always welcomed and included newcomers. We felt good about that. But we were not in the top tier. That included mostly town kids whose fathers were professionals or businessmen and well-to-do. My mother, a practical nurse, ,made 200 plus dollars a month in her full time job, and we lived in the country.

For the annual May Day celebration, the student body selected a court with a queen and several princesses. Everybody knew who would be on the court each year. But this year the top clique—and I— were the selected ones! I was of course, surprised and thrilled.

At the next assembly, several of the popular group said to me, "Come sit with us," and they made room for me in their row. It was a nice gesture though. I felt uncomfortable, but squeezed in among them and immediately regretted it. I was out of place. There were my friends up ahead, and I wasn't among them. I wondered what they were thinking.

For the May Day program we wore pretty, strapless light green formals made of dotted Swiss with bouffant skirts that whirled gracefully. We each picked an escort,

165

and the couples did a choreographed waltz to the beautiful, romantic song, "I'll be with you in apple blossom time." All but me. I was so religious, I didn't dance and followed the path of others I'd seen in former years, my escort and I standing to the side looking holier than thou while the others did the lovely dance.

I felt good to have been chosen. But I knew that it was the glen plaid skirt that earned me that recognition. Without it I wouldn't have qualified.

That skirt was made out of such great fabric that it still looked like new at the end of its well-worn year. It had done its job, and I almost never wore it after that. Probably it was out of style by then. I don't know where it ended up, but I remember it fondly. It taught me something.

I learned that what you have doesn't make you who you are even though it may affect how others see you. My skirt taught me that you need to be of good fabric too, and that you shouldn't depend on what you have, to give you value. It doesn't turn you into a different person.

After that one assembly when I sat with the elites, I eagerly went back to my old friends. Proof of their true friendship was that they didn't seem to notice that I'd been away.

I remembered one of Mrs. Wilson's corny Memory Gems that she made us memorize and recite in grade school. "Make new friends, but keep the old; these are silver; those are gold."

Corny but true. And that year it took on meaning.

SOCIALLY CHALLENGED

29

I never learned any real social skills when I was a child nor as I grew up. Around the family, I think I was all right, but of course they're the ones I didn't learn any social skills from. Outside of that, I usually didn't even know when to laugh. For a period of time in my life, I would laugh whenever everybody else did, just because it appeared to be the thing to do. I gradually gained some confidence in my own judgment of humor and quit laughing just as a pretense.

Going to the Emmanuel Baptist Church until I was grown, I was taught that very little that most people do socially was appropriate, or allowed, for good Christians. You weren't supposed to dance, drink, smoke (though many of the men did, the minute they got out of the church), play cards, go to shows, or use the Lord's name in vain. My family went to shows anyway, feeling no guilt. My dad didn't go to church, but Mom took my brother and me every Sunday and occasionally in between.

Maybe I would have done better if I'd picked up on my dad's attitude. He was not so strict about these behaviors. I think he used to dance as a young man, and wasn't opposed to accepting a drink just to be polite. Though we never had alcohol in the house because Mom wouldn't allow it. I never saw him drink any except a sip or two once or twice when some logger friends brought some in and poured him one. He never finished one of those drinks. After they were gone, one of us would take it for him and pour the rest of it in the sink. He said, "I just drink a little because they brought it in for me. To be polite." He of course knew Mama's opinion about drinking, and was just trying to reassure me.

I was reassured. It didn't bother me anyway. Mama didn't say anything about it either. But she did point out to me that Daddy didn't drink enough to speak of. Somebody had given him a fifth of whiskey one time, and she showed me where he kept it. In a hole in an old myrtle tree out in back. I'm sure that was because she wouldn't allow it in the house. But also she mentioned that it had been there for five years, and it was still almost full.

On the other hand, I came home from school one day, hungry as always, and opened the refrigerator. This is when Daddy was sick in bed. I don't know where Mama was, but at least not there in the kitchen. I did a double-take. I couldn't believe my eyes. There it was. A carton. Of beer.

I was stunned. That was almost worse than the hard stuff. That's how well I'd been taught, by the Baptist Church, and by Mama I guess. I looked at it and thought, "Whose could it be?" It was as if my life had been toppled.

Could it belong to Uncle Guy? I didn't know if he drank beer. He didn't go to church. If it was his, why was it in our refrigerator? I was too shocked to mention it to anybody. I couldn't ask. I simply could not fathom who it could belong to or why it would be there.

Maybe Mama thought I would wonder about that, because she brought it up a little later. "Oh, I bought Daddy some beer. He said he thought a cold beer sounded good, so I got him some. What a relief. It made sense, and I should have known Mama was not that extreme. He was sick, and it was increasingly hard to find anything that he could tolerate. The mystery was solved. And it wasn't nearly as cataclysmic as I'd thought. I think he tried one, and it didn't taste as good as he'd thought it might. So the rest of it disappeared soon. I don't know where it went.

Daddy was moderate in all things except smoking. He was addicted to that and knew it was bad for him. "Don't ever do it. You can see what it's done to me," as he lit up another one.

My brother and I obediently followed the church's edicts. We didn't dance, smoke, drink, swear, or play cards, and weren't really tempted to, except for Old Maid and Authors. But that was okay because it wasn't gambling.

"Playing cards"—the ones with clubs, kings, and queens—were sinful whether there was money involved or not. I don't know if the Bible says it's a sin to play cards. I doubt if they had them when the Bible was written. Our church took everything in the Bible literally, except where it says to take a little wine for thy stomach's sake, or describes where Jesus turned the water into wine. In my church they said it didn't really mean wine; it meant grape juice.

Which reminds me of hearing about some teenage protestant, deciding he was going to be a Catholic because you could do anything you want to.

You just go to confession and your sins are washed away. It wasn't that easy for the Baptists.

From time to time I have been invited to play cards with friends, or to dance. I was never interested in card-playing, and couldn't seem to learn it when Canasta was the rage. But dancing could have been fun. I always had to decline because I didn't know how. I just said, "I don't dance."

That probably sounded self-righteous, and I think it was probably embarrassing to the person asking because it sounded like an excuse. It didn't happen often because I wasn't asked that often. But when it did I don't think they believed me. The worst was when a couple of African American boys asked me to dance. A group of us Phi Beta girls from the U of O (Phi Beta, being a music and drama honorary) made several trips to Fort Lewis to entertain the troops coming home from Korea, and I couldn't agree to dance. It had nothing to do with them. It was my inferiority and lack of social skills, thanks to the Baptist church.

A couple of times, after I was grown, I did give in to dance when some more self-assured man wouldn't take no for an answer. In both cases they were strong dancers, and almost made me look like I knew what I was doing because they took the bull by the horns, so to speak, and whirled me around the room with abandon.

Similarly I was always uncomfortable in a situation where people were having drinks—in the days when it was not socially acceptable to decline alcohol, and people would insist that you have one, call you a party pooper, and give you one anyway. I have never developed a taste for alcohol. I don't even like pop. But I felt unsophisticated; I wouldn't have known what to order if I'd wanted a drink. At last, with relief, I no longer concern myself with sophistication. And I still don't drink.

I also never learned to make small talk, and it bored me. I love talking to someone about something, but I still am not entertained by small talk and have never developed the talent.

In fact I grew up mostly never knowing what to say in much of any social situation, and could go through a whole date barely speaking. I still don't know how I was lucky enough to have a second date and somehow get to the point of marriage. After I got more self-confidence and to my great relief, began thinking of something to say, a couple of times I had some man tell me I talked too much.

Which reminds me of Jonathon Winters. He said, "You go through life, and they tell you, 'You're too young. You're too young.' Then all of sudden, 'You're too old'."

I can relate to that too.

30

When Mel and I were in Scotland in 1960 we saw the Finley tartan and coat of arms. So there really is a clan. Since then I learned that Macbeth was one of our forebears, and Inverness was our castle. I think I am the only one who finds that particularly interesting. When I mention it, nobody responds. Or they yawn.

On the internet I saw mention of the fact that the Finley clan was outlawed at some point, but they didn't say when. Or why.

Without thought to any of that, we always referred to our family as the Finley clan. I suppose because we were clannish. We mostly lived within a few miles of each other, all living respectable lives. I thought I had the best relatives anywhere.

Down the road a quarter of a mile, my mother's parents, Grandma and Grandpa, Edwin Benjamin and Genarah Katherine Finley, lived. They had several acres with huge gardens, fields for cows, barn, chickens, a creek, and Old Pronto, an old tired work horse. The family always called it, "The place."

The house, small but nice, was a craftsman bungalow with the porch around two sides, four bedrooms, two up and two down, living room with fireplace, lath squares on the ceiling, and colonnades separating the living from the dining room. A bathroom with a claw foot tub and always a big bucket of cactus soap they'd ordered from Texas. It had a pleasant, delicate fragrance, pale green with a gelatinous consistency. You dipped your fingers into it and used it to wash your hands. I washed my hands a lot when I was at Grandma's. Then the kitchen with a wood stove and room for a little drop leaf table and chairs where we had breakfast when we happened to be there. Oatmeal with rich cream and sugar, and hot biscuits with butter and quince jelly, the most memorable. Just outside, at the end of the porch was the fruit room, always full of canned fruits and vegetables that they'd grown.

I remember helping Grandpa slash dried beans out of their husks outside. He scraped apple and fed it to us when we were little. That means you cut an apple in half and then scrape the pulp out of it a bite at a time with a teaspoon. He called the little kids "Monkey Jo" and ate cookies at the kitchen sink, sticking them under the cold running water each time he took a bite. Grandma was a good cook, but I remember her cookies being kind of dry and hard. Maybe that's why he did that. Some cookies are good that way. Something like dunking donuts.

On occasion, some of the kids stayed overnight at their house, just for fun. Once Betty and Susan, a friend Ramona, and I stayed in the two upstairs bedrooms when we were preteens, having a lot of fun, running back and forth between the rooms. Grandpa finally came to the bottom of the stairs, and called up, "You kids hesh up up there." (Yes, it was "hesh". He grew up in Arkansas.)

173

That's as strict as he ever got, and it was all that was necessary.

My mother adored him. He was a wonderful father I know. Mom was probably a lot like him, the calmer of her parents. Except one time when she was very irritated with me. Probably because she wanted some help, and I was fooling around outside. I was a little too old to spank I think, probably eleven, and I'd only had one of those when I was two, and I believe Mama had Daddy give it to me because I'd gone out in the road.

But another time, when I was a lot older, too old for spankings, Mama was pretty upset. I was standing by the bike, and she came striding over to me, obviously intending to give me a spat. So I jumped away, around the bike, she came around the other way, and I jumped the other way. Finally she gave up. And I suppose I went and did what she wanted.

That reminded me of Grandma telling about when Aunt Verna was little, and she was trying to give her a dose of salts. That seemed to be the cure for everything back then. "I tried to get her to take it, and she wouldn't, and I tried again, and she wouldn't. I kept trying to get her to take it, and she wouldn't. So I just drank it myself and went on."

I never stopped to wonder how Grandpa and Grandma got a much nicer house than ours. They were dirt farmers with some farm animals, so the income was conservative and mostly seasonal. I learned later though that when they got the house, it wasn't completely finished. And Aunt Verna still lived at home with them, teaching school. She had a big part in their getting the house, and bought most of

174

the furniture, a nice mohair couch and chair with rounded arms for one thing. I later learned that my dad and Uncle Cince had each supplied them with some money every month as well, for years.

Uncle Cince, (Cincinnatus), Mom's just younger brother, and Aunt Eunice, with daughter Glennis and son Cecil, lived right across the road from them in a cute house built in the 20s. It had an arched doorway or two, 3 bedrooms, formal dining plus a built-in dinette in the kitchen, a modern bathroom, central heating from a wood furnace in the basement with a vent in the hall to let the heat up. The basement was also a garage and had an open shower. They had concrete walks, and what we would now call a patio in back. Uncle Cince, the most well-to-do in the family was a long time used car salesman, and eventually owned the Ford Garage in Coquille with a partner.

Glen Aiken Road ran off Highway 42, halfway up to our house. Uncle Zed, Mom's youngest sibling and Aunt Selma with their four, Pudgy (Ronald), (He was adopted because they couldn't seem to have one of their own, but then they had three more.) Baby (Diane), Katie, and Mike, and they lived a mile or so up that road in a little house in a valley. Uncle Zed was a blacksmith.

On up Hwy 42 around a curve, Uncle Guy, the eldest sibling, and Aunt Nota lived with their sons, Darrell and Freddie. That was just across the road and a few yards below our place. Uncle Guy worked at the Smith Woods plywood mill in Coquille for years, driving their old Model a Ford for most of that time.

Every winter, the Coquille River overflowed just

175

beyond "the place" and Uncle Cince's. It covered the road, for days so that you couldn't drive through. And a way beyond us, it covered the road as well, so we were stranded for a while, as if on an island, unable to get to town or to work. My favorite time each year. Everyone was home together. Sometimes the relatives and neighbors mingled from house to house, and Dads were home. We played games, ate, went down to the river to look at the high water. There was always something to talk about. It was like one big party each year until they made changes in the roads and ruined it.

One year during high water, Boyd's wife Ruby was having one of her babies so needed to get through to the hospital. Fortunately, by then they had brought in an army "duck", an amphibious vehicle made to prevail over deep water, so they took her to town in that. Prior to the duck days, I don't know what people did in emergencies. I didn't worry too much about emergencies then, and ever since, I've loved times of adversity best. Like snow days when there's no school. But then our ecosystem wasn't yet starting to flounder.

Aunt Verna, the youngest sister, and Uncle Darrell with their four, Sonny (Darrell), Virginia, Edwin, and Emory, lived in town. Aunt Verna taught elementary school and Uncle Darrell was a house painter who always wore neatly ironed white shirts, some of them reflecting colorful indications of his line of work.

When we were little, we called Aunt Verna, Aunt Bunny. Wish I knew where that came from.

Part of the time Aunt Bessie, Mom's other sister, and

Uncle George with their five—Wilfred, Susan, Betty, Georgie, and Johnny, lived in town. They moved quite a bit—to Chemawa, an Indian school near Salem, and to a farm house near Salem. Then back to Glen Aiken Road. Aunt Bessie was a teacher too. Uncle George was a timber cruiser. He also worked on Indian causes as he was half Native American Indian, and made trips to Washington, DC where he had some success in getting land allotted back to the Indians.

The only one missing was Uncle Hugh (Elihu). He was a little more adventurous, living in Panama for some time, and was a painter for the first painting of the new Golden Gate Bridge. Prior to that he'd been a high climber in the woods in Oregon, which entailed climbing a tall, straight tree, denuded of its limbs, with a rope and spiked boots, going up and sawing off the top of the tree and hooking in cables to assist in pulling other fallen trees up to a loading spot. I heard of men racing to get to the top and not looking up soon enough, so throwing their rope over and falling to their deaths. That was one of the most dangerous, and admired jobs in the woods at the time.

He was married to Alta Lowell, and had a daughter Nola. They eventually divorced and he married Myrtle, a pretty nurse whom he adored, but she died at a young age. He married once more, to Birdie, who was with him when he died in his fifties in about 1948 back home in Oregon.

I think I was the first one in the clan to graduate from college. Then Wilfred and Georgie, in the Wasson family, and Sonny, Virginia, and Edwin, the Coxes, also did. Wilfred and Georgie got Doctorates and did some teaching in higher education plus working on the Indian causes. Virginia worked at a research lab at the U of O, Edwin taught school for years, and Sonny is a lawyer in California.

We saw all the nearby relatives on a regular basis, dropping in on each other almost daily. The big get-togethers were the fun times though. They always happened on holidays, family picnics and trips to Bandon when we borrowed Dr. Richmond's beach house for a few nights.

But in between were the drop in visits. Uncle Cince and Aunt Eunice seemed to dote on me.

Uncle Zed wasn't particularly interested in me until I got a little older and learned to play "Bumble Boogie". He wouldn't take no for an answer. I always had to play it for him when he came. Then later he wanted to hear Christy play Ave Maria on her cello, demanding to hear it every time she had it with her. If the boys had been making their records in his lifetime, I'm sure he would have loved their jazz. Too bad he missed that. Others in the family were musical, the sisters and Uncle Cince sang and played the piano, but never Uncle Zed. Yet he's the one who seemed to appreciate hearing our music the most.

Except for the time Christy was going to play at the Baptist Church. We were going to do Ave Maria, it is so beautiful, and one of her special pieces. But Brother Charlie, the preacher, said "No" to that because it was Catholic. It wasn't appropriate for Baptists. Uncle Cince and Brother Charlie kind of had it out over that. Brother Charlie won.

Aunt Nota walked up every day to get the mail. All the mail boxes were together nearest our house. She usually stopped by to say hello, always wearing her heavy cotton stockings. She was sweet, and very pretty, but a little odd and wouldn't come in and stay awhile, just stood by the door for a few minutes.

She asked me when I was about eight if I would like to make my mother some dish towels to surprise her for her birthday. She provided some for me and showed me how to embroider them, which I did at her house so it would be a surprise for Mama. What a thoughtful idea. Sometimes she brought us a dish of her delicious homemade cottage cheese. Most people in the world have never tasted real cottage cheese. Just that stuff with guar gum and who knows what else in it that you buy in stores. Even the "natural" kind. We had only raw milk in those days. That may have had something to do with it.

Every Friday evening, "like clockwork," Mama and Daddy said, we saw Uncle Guy and Aunt Nota driving to town with the kids, in the Model A, to the Liberty to see whatever was on at the show. "You could set your clock by them."

One day Mom was telling about some guy who told a story that ended, "That's one time I was stumped." Uncle Guy added, "As if a man wasn't stumped every day of his life."

Aunt Bessie called me "Sis". She was warm and friendly and provided a rich, loving environment for her kids. She liked music and sang and played the piano, as did her sisters and Uncle Cince. Most of it was reading the

179

treble clef, and chording with the left hand. Occasionally you'd hear a discord. Mom had had some lessons, and played just hymns, note by note. For some reason she always hit the left hand just ahead of the right. They all had their idiosyncrasies. All of them sang too.

Aunt Verna always had something funny to say. Like, "There's a place for everything in this house. And it's right here in this drawer." She quit going to church in later years though Uncle Darrell continued. Someone asked why he kept going without her, and she said, "He need it."

She was always losing something, and she'd say, "It's just hunt, hunt, hunt," emphasizing every "h".

She also broke lots of dishes. "Those dishes aren't any good," she'd say, "They just didn't hold up." And she burned most of what she baked. She was Mom's youngest sister, and Mom said, "Verna's just harum, scarum. She always has been."

As her 50th wedding anniversary approached and they were planning a celebration, she declared in a high pitched voice, "I'm going to lose weight if they have to carry me in on a stretcher!" We all laughed.

Uncle Darrell, Aunt Verna's husband, was softer spoken, but he was funny too. Once when a bunch of the relatives were together at Mom's house after I was grown and married, the women had collected in the kitchen, and the men were in the living room. We'd made cookies, and thought we should take some in to the men. I decided it would be quaint to serve them from an antique chamber pot that Mom had sitting on a counter. So I filled it up and carried it around the room to each of the men in succession.

Mel, clearly alert, said, "Why not?" and took one. Everybody took some, but most didn't notice or weren't going to give me the satisfaction of acknowledging the unusual container. I doubt if my brother noticed. He just took a cookie and kept talking. Probably too absent-minded.

When I got to Uncle Darrell, he took one and said, kind of confidentially, "Would you ask your mother if she uses this for ever-day or just for good?"

Our family had so much fun. I grew up thinking we had the most perfect family in the world.

Probably not.

But I'll bet an improvement over that Macbeth bunch.

CHRISTMAS PAST

31

The first and only time I heard the caroling was when I was eleven. The soft full tones seeped into my consciousness, waking me from deep sleep, and sounding like angels from heaven. The next year I joined the group, and Christmas was never the same again.

It was Aunt Verna, who decided the family should go caroling on Christmas mornings. The first year, 1923, she was still a teenager and recruited a sister and 2 brothers to make up the quartet that started the Finley family tradition.

They selected a song from an old shape notes hymnal called Harvest Bells that my grandfather had used when he taught "Singing School" years before in Arkansas. It was called "Song of the Angels" and used the lyrics of "It Came Upon a Midnight Clear" but with a different tune from the popular carol of today, and had a chorus—"Roll on, glad song, O'er earth's wide realm again. We'll join the glad refrain of peace on earth, good will to men." They moved into "Silent Night" without a break, and that is all they ever sang.

Each year more of the family joined in, and the over-40-year tradition was well-established by the time I started participating in 1943.

The family, all the kids and grandkids of my

grandparents, Ed and Genarah Finley, would gather every year for a festive Christmas Eve at their house where we ate sandwiches, cookies, nuts and candy canes, exchanged presents, marveled at the huge fir sparkling with ancient decorations, and practiced our songs, making sure we had a good balance of sopranos, altos, tenors, and basses for our 4-part renditions. Sometimes Grandpa made popcorn, he had grown, in his wire mesh popper with the long handle, shaking it in the blazing fireplace.

It was at the same fireplace that some of us, when we were little, had dictated a note to Santa Claus, before Christmas, that Grandpa or Grandma wrote for us. Then we held it in the fireplace, over the fire, let go, and the draft sucked it right up the chimney and on to the North Pole. A magical thing.

And it was in that living room when Bette was four, I five, and Susan six, that Santa Claus came in. Bette and I were thrilled. But Susan, the smart one, said, "Oh, there isn't such a thing as Santa Claus. That's Cecil. Can't you see that? There's no Santa Claus." Betty and I were incensed. "There is too." We argued about it, but we ended up disillusioned and mad at Susan for ruining Christmas.

Then it was home for a few hours of sleep for the carolers before they got up at 2 or 3 AM, bundled up against the freezing cold, and piled into 2 or 3 cars to head out for caroling.

We were serious about it. Any talking was in whispers, and there was no audible laughing nor slamming of car doors, no Jingle Bells, Good King Wenceslas, nor horsing around. We went to houses of people we knew, that we

183

thought would appreciate it, and gathered under bedroom windows to sing until dawn.

Times were different then, and Coquille was a small town of about 4000. The population hasn't grown. It's remained that size for the next seventy years. But these days we would probably be arrested or shot, sneaking around houses in the middle of the night anywhere. At that time few of us even had a key to lock our doors.

People clicked their lights on and off to let us know they heard, and we walked away, fading out on the last phrase of "Silent Night" so they could fall back asleep.

After caroling we always went to one of our houses for a pre-arranged breakfast and to wind down before we broke up and went home.

At age one hundred and two, my mother still remembered going home after caroling for four or five hours and cooking Christmas dinner while the rest of us napped. It is easy to understand why she couldn't keep up with that. Also after my father died in 1945 she had to get a job so stopped going caroling.

As the years went on, some music-loving friends joined us. For most of them once was enough. My brother wrote in his story about the carolers: "After one session most of them went away convinced the Finleys had to be mad to get out of warm beds to face such punishment." We had numb feet but warm hearts.

After my mother came home one Christmas morning from her graveyard nursing shift, she entered the house to find several strange men stretched out sound asleep on her living room floor. Then she recognized one as the local

Catholic Priest, a unique ecumenical moment in that Baptist household. She was surprised, but they looked quite comfortable so she said, "I just stepped over the priest and went on in the kitchen to start cooking Christmas dinner."

It isn't as if we never had any fun. We always caroled to the patients at the Knife Hospital, named after its owner, Belle Knife, who everybody called Aunt Belle.

We never decided ahead of time whether we would sing one or two verses of each song so we were always well into the first verse when somebody would stick up one finger suggesting one verse, or two fingers for two. That always worked. Except once in the hospital, in the well-lit hall, somebody stuck up one finger, and this time another one argued the point by sticking up 2. Various ones joined in the argument, as we continued to sing, and Uncle Darrell, with his wry sense of humor, finally stuck up one finger, bent at the knuckle, suggesting half a verse. That settled it as some of us crumbled into laughter, unable to continue, and we faded out a little early that time. They still let us in in future years in spite of that, but I'm not sure why.

Of course everybody in town couldn't hear us—only the 20 or so we got to each year, and maybe some of their close neighbors, but the Finley family caroling became well-known in the area— sort of a Coquille answer to the Von Trapps. Many said to us over the years, often with tearful eyes, that it wouldn't seem like Christmas without it.

It never seemed quite like Christmas to us either after the custom stopped. Some had gotten too old, or thought they were, and others moved away as times changed.

Occasionally some cousin in a fit of nostalgia still calls another one at 3 or 4 AM on Christmas morning and starts singing "Song of the Angels" in our older, raspier voices. The callee, of course, enters in without hesitation, harmonizing until laughter overcomes us.

We never expected anything for the caroling; we just hoped to share some of the pleasure in the spirit of Christmas. Mrs. Oerding had a gift-wrapped box of chocolates for us every year, and occasionally somebody made us a batch of fudge, which we couldn't turn down.

But the most touching tribute we ever had was when the wonderful poet and family friend, Frances Holmstrom wrote about us. She was the mother of the once famous Buzz Holmstrom who was the first person to navigate the wild Colorado River, a trip we watched on newsreels

Years later, after he had died, at his own hand, his homemade boat which he built for the trip still sat crumbling in the weeds of the yard by her little weathered house where we stood to carol.

This is what she wrote:

TO CAROLERS UNDER MY WINDOW

Oh, on this Christmas morning, ere the lamps of town went out,

As the foggy dark was paling, The Angels were about.

They were about and singing, and through the leafless tree

With joyful tidings winging, the song came up to me.

Though dun their dark disguise was, it was not hard to guess

That under the long topcoats was celestial loveliness

And the heavenly song that waked me with its news of "Peace, Goodwill,"

Was that which first stirred shepherds watching sheep upon the hill.

They were incarnate voices: like slowly turned out flame,

Both song and singer melted as softly as they came

Into the dripping dawn-mist—and as there shown a light

About the kneeling shepherds on that far distant night,

So all my heart was lumined by the message, Christmas morn

Of those who went forth singing because their Christ was born.

32

My only sibling. My brother.

The big oval-framed picture of him always decorated a wall in our house. Even as a young baby he had black hair and dark brown eyes, like our dad. He sat snug in a white wicker buggy, which, come to think of it, I never saw in reality. What could have happened to it? Mom was good at parting with things. She didn't like clutter. I wouldn't put it past her to have disposed of anything that size in their little house after he grew too big for it. But it was a beautiful item, much too nice to part with. Oh, to have one of those now.

After all I didn't come along for another seven and a half years, a long time to save something just in case, and which probably came as a surprise to them anyway.

Mama told me about what a long and difficult birth his was, and how he had a series of convulsions soon after, scaring them half to death, I'm sure making him even more precious to them. When I came along, it was quick and easy. Maybe I didn't earn the respect he seemed to have. I felt like more of a joke.

When he started to school, Glennis, our cousin, two years Boyd's senior, said she interpreted for him at school because he couldn't talk plain enough for the teacher to understand him.

I got the impression that Boyd didn't do very well in school. But by the time I was able to understand English, he talked plain enough for me. In later years he said he was always hard of hearing. That's why he couldn't talk plain. And he couldn't hear the teacher. Apparently nobody was aware of that. They may have just thought he was a little slow.

My brother seemed to lack self-confidence. But he was good-looking and I know girls found him attractive. He probably never enjoyed that. I don't think he knew it.

I admired my big brother. He had interesting activities and possessions, like the collection of Big Little Books and the red wooden tool box full of Valentines and other valuables that I got to go through once in a while. There was a colorful tin train on a track that went through tunnels on its 12-inch oval when you wound it up.

All I remember having then of my own besides some story books, were color books and crayons. Well, another doll every year and a miniature tea set. A trike and a wagon. I did have some things. But his always seemed more interesting.

He made airplanes out of balsa wood models, spreading out newspaper on the table where he glued the pieces together while I sat on the other side and watched, and sniffed the glue when he wasn't using it. It had a cold, silvery smell, and I loved it. Mom said a few times, "I don't think you ought to smell that so much. It might not be good for you." She was ahead of her time. Nobody had ever thought of it being harmful that I know of. I did it a little less of it but didn't cut it out altogether.

Fortunately that wasn't a daily activity. Maybe the rarity of it saved me from serious addiction and too much brain damage. Sometime later that glue was legally banned. I was a little disappointed at hearing that. Only years later did I learn about kids sniffing airplane glue and all kinds of things that got them high, like gasoline. Maybe that was the glue they talked about. I never noticed any change in myself though. I just liked its smell.

Before I started to school, Boyd used to read to me. We'd climb into Mama and Daddy's bed in the mornings, probably on weekends or in summer, where he read me books and then entertained me, making up airplane stories with sound effects, keeping me enthralled for what seemed like hours 'til Mama put a stop to it. I think we were both disappointed because it was a lot of fun for us. He was a good storyteller, and I was a good audience. But she probably thought it was inappropriate. Who knows?

Beyond that we didn't have much of a relationship during our childhoods except his grouching at me because I was always doing something annoying. He always worried, about everything, and complained at me more than anything else.

I probably deserved it. One time, the only time I remember that I know I deserved it was when we were at Grandma and Grandpa's house, out in the front yard. He was playing with a ball, dribbling and catching it. I wanted to get in on it, he was having so much fun. I really just wanted him to toss it to me or bounce it to me. But he

190

didn't, so I started whining and trying to cry, for him to give me the ball. Mama heard it and, I'm sure not knowing what else to do, ordered, "Boyd, give her that ball." That's as cranky as she ever got. He threw it down in disgust. Suddenly my desire for the ball evaporated. It lay on the ground, fallow. I felt sorry for my brother and appropriately guilty. That's the only time I remember acting like that and whining for something.

In high school Boyd went out for track, played a tuba in the band, and sang in the chorus. All of this seemed magical and highly accomplished to me. He liked to sing and had a beautiful voice, sitting on the floor by the radio every Saturday night, singing along with the Hit Parade.

Boyd loved cars and learned to drive off road before he was old enough for a license. When he was sixteen he bought a Model T Ford coupe for $13.75, painted it yellow and spent a lot of time working on it. He always seemed to like working on old cars. Later, picked up other classic cars from time to time, like a black Cord roadster with a Jaguar body, that didn't get much driving because he wasn't sure it was safe. He was fascinated with mechanics and different types of vehicles.

When I was in college I gave him a book about the Stanley Steamer which he seemed to like better than any other present I ever gave him. He read it several times and has brought it up many times over the next 60 years, excitedly telling me about some of the details of that invention, which mostly escaped me—both my interest and my understanding. But I'm glad I found the right present.

Immediately after they graduated from high school,

Boyd and our cousin Wilfred joined the Army Air Corp. The principal, Mr. Osika helped postpone their draft into the army, allowing them to graduate and then join the Air Corps. They had to be above average for that; Boyd said in one of his stories later that that was the only time in his life, he was "above average", thanks to Mr. Osika. They went to Fort Lewis in Washington State for induction, and to Wichita Falls, Texas, for basic training.

Then they went separate ways. Boyd to Indianapolis for pilot training. He decided against being a pilot after he watched another trainee crash his plane on his first solo. It scared him, and he wasn't one to exercise false bravado. There were plenty of other jobs in the Air Corps. Others "washed out" because they didn't exhibit the skills required.

Wilfred became a tail-gunner in the European arena, and received a purple heart. He was called "Geronimo" by his buddies because he was Indian, and looked like it, even though he was just a quarter. As kids, Boyd and Wilfred used to play cowboys and Indians. Boyd was always the Indian.

To tide myself over through this period, I bought a copy of the sheet music for The Army Air Corps song, and played and sang it daily. And I went to see Ronald Reagan in *This is the Army*, several times. (Well, I was only 12.) It was my favorite movie for a long time. And also, I'll admit, I had a crush on Ronald Reagan. But I got over that.

Boyd had a leave before shipping overseas so came home for a short visit. Daddy had been sick in bed for some time by then. Boyd, at 20, was leaving for an unknown

192

period. We all said goodbye. He went to Daddy and held out his hand to him. Daddy said, "You'd better kiss me." I knew why. Boyd kissed him goodbye and went out the door.

Boyd sent most of his meager pay home to us every month. I got a pittance from babysitting, but I just spent that on myself.

When Dr. Richmond saw that Daddy didn't have much time left, Mom with some help, contacted the Red Cross to run interference and get Boyd discharged early. The war had ended by then. After most of his service in New Guinea and a while in the Philippines, he was sent to Japan. The order came through for his early discharge so we looked forward to his arrival at home.

We were provided with a copy of the letter Dr. Richmond had written to them. It said that Daddy had about three months to live.

Mom showed it to Daddy and me. I said, trying to soften that news for him, and because I was in denial, "He just said that to help get Boyd home sooner." Daddy said, "No, he means it."

He was right. Daddy died about three months later. Boyd didn't make it home for almost four months after that. He said he thought some sergeant had intentionally interfered with his discharge as ordered.

He got home three days before Christmas. We did our traditional early Christmas morning caroling, always numbing cold. That continued for many more years. Boyd said that first time back, he thought he was more miserable than any time he'd spent in the war.

We heard some stories about his experience overseas. But the consensus was that you shouldn't ask. Many of the soldiers didn't like to talk about it when they came home.

He had sent Mom a present, that he'd bought in New Guinea or Australia, a little wool mat with a kangaroo on it. He was surprised when he got home and saw it because what he had paid for was a large, nice area rug. He did tell us about some interesting places and people, the natives in New Guinea, and Australia, and some descriptions of the war itself, with strafing attacks during Japanese air raids, and hiding in foxholes. In his tent he once found a huge lizard camping under his cot.

His typing classes in high school paid off because one day when they asked for somebody who could type, he was the only one who raised his hand, and they gave him the job. Much of the time he drove a truck, hauling soldiers from place to place. And once drove a tired and disheveled Bob Hope from his plane to another show on his annual tour for the armed services.

I was 14 by the time he was back home so we had more in common than we'd ever had before. I played the piano, and we sang, sometimes we went to a show together, and we sang in the church choir.

He got a job at Smith Woods plywood mill, the major business in Coquille, and ended up working there for 41 years through some changes of hands, and with just a few breaks when they were closed for strikes. He always stayed employed though, by buying a power mower and mowing lawns during a couple of those breaks. Other times he drove a milk truck, picking up from the dairies and

194

delivering to the creamery.

Boyd had a couple of girlfriends, and then met Ruby Casey, a pretty young woman, who he became engaged to and married. I was thrilled about that. I'd always wanted a sister. Here she was. But I eventually figured out that she didn't share my enthusiasm. She had other sisters and didn't need me. She had a four year old boy, Terry, from a former marriage, who was so cute and sweet. I loved him. Boyd built him a tree house in one of the old Improved Northern Spy apple trees Daddy had planted, and taught him to read, starting by labeling items around the house. And then they had three more children, Sharon, Marilyn, and Johnny, whom I also loved.

They rented a little old house for a while that my aunt owned, and then moved into the living quarters that had been built onto the back of the service station for some of its renters. They started thinking about a house of their own, and Mom agreed to sign over most of her three acres to them, putting my name on her house and its .39 of an acre with a life estate for herself. They decided on a house plan.

He bought an old commercial building in town, had it torn down and moved the parts onto the acreage. I watched him, before his afternoon shift at the mill, every day, standing for hours, pulling nails out of the lumber, stacking it, and getting equipped to build. Ruby said, "It will never happen." He kept going. This went on for five years. The picture of persistence. He got help laying the foundation, and a few other features such as wiring and cabinetry, but he did most of the carpentry work himself.

195

They had picked out the model they wanted, and somehow he did it. Mom said, "Boyd never could drive a nail straight." She thought his left-handedness hindered him that way. We were amazed that he was able to accomplish all that.

When it was finished, it was all paid for. He's never had a mortgage. I think he doesn't approve of mortgages. I kind of agree, having been responsible for paying them for years.

Their house, probably 1800 square feet, is a three-bedroom, two-bath with living room, formal dining room, eat-in kitchen, large laundry room, double garage, and a hip roof. A fireplace in the living room, and hardwood floors throughout. It is a beautiful, well-built house. Then he later built a patio in back and dug a swimming pool by hand, with shovels, and with the help of the kids. He thought it would be a nice family project. It was about 12 feet long by eight feet wide (my guess) and full of fresh water that flowed through a little rock-lined stream they built. But it was ice cold so it didn't get much use. The only time I saw anybody in it was when Mel, my husband, decided to give it a try. He dove in and immediately back up, shivering and managed to utter in a tremulous voice, "By George, that's cold!" as he climbed out. It gave Boyd and me a good laugh. It was an accomplishment though, and a good, creative effort.

That wasn't all my brother did that surprised me. After he retired from the mill where he had done almost all the jobs there at one time or another and ended up being the oiler, keeping the machinery running, he took up another

196

venture.

One of my mother's cousins, Kurt Beckham, a former school teacher, had been writing historical columns for the Myrtle Point Herald for years. He got older and retired from that. Boyd wrote an article and submitted it. They liked it, and asked for more. So he wrote for the Myrtle Point Herald and the Coquille Sentinel, one column a week for years. It seemed a completely foreign kind of thing for him to do. But his stories were good with lots of humor. He just seemed to have a natural knack for it, and people liked his stories. They are actually more entertaining than Kurt's. He did extensive research and interviewing of old-timers in Coos County, always enjoying talking to people and was interested in the history of the area anyway so it worked out well. He did it just for his own pleasure, and that of others. They offered to pay him, but he declined.

Strangely he seemed to just know how to write. He does things to make a good story that I never heard of until I started reading books on writing when I was 79, and taking workshops to learn. I went to college. He didn't. But I never had any instruction on writing in school, either high school or college. And neither did he.

After a few years, he put together four collections of his articles into books, and later compiled all of them, with some additions, into a larger book. They've all sold, and he's had to reorder several times. All he wanted was to break even on his cost. A school counselor in North Carolina wrote to him, he answered, and an ongoing correspondence was established. She eventually came to Oregon with her boyfriend to see Boyd. She wanted to meet him. He has calls from people all around the country about his books. These far away people have some connection with Coos County or Oregon, but it's still rather amazing.

One year when I was delivering Meals on Wheels to seniors in Springfield, I went into a lady's house and saw her reading a book that looked just like one of Boyd's. It WAS one of Boyd's. She had three of them. I thought even that was surprising, way up here in Lane County.

I wrote a Christmas letter once that used his story about our family caroling tradition, and in the introduction, I wrote that my brother, "an unlikely writer" had written it. He thought that was funny, and prefaced his last book with a list of things that people had said about him—"An unlikely writer"—"Down to earth"—"Straight forward"— "Simple without adornment"—"Interesting"—Hard to put down"—"Human interest stories with meat behind them"— "He writes just like he talks"—"Marvelously readable, at times humorous, at times poignant, but always engaging"— "I like his endings." Boyd added, "Then there was the fellow-worker at Georgia-Pacific who wanted the world to know by writing a letter to the Editor of The Coquille Valley Sentinel, that he had worked with Boyd Stone for 27 years and 'was surprised he could write anything.' Oh well, you can't win them all."

Through those last years, Boyd took on another whole persona. He is now considered the Coos County Historian and has received some recognition for that. The Coos County Historical Association presented him a plaque, honoring him for his contribution to county history. People who want to know anything in that realm are sent to him, or many call him first. He rode with his wife in a float one year, as Grand Marshall of a Coquille celebration. I didn't see it, but I'm sure he enjoyed waving to all the admiring civilians.

A few years ago a retired editor of one of New York's prestigious papers, came to Coquille and became the editor of the Sentinel for a few years. One day a man came into the Sentinel office with a question. The attendant at the desk went back to ask the editor if he knew the answer. He said, "Tell them to contact Boyd Stone." She said, "It IS Boyd Stone." He came out to shake his hand. "So you're Boyd Stone! I'm so glad to meet you. I love your writing!" I think Boyd felt like that was the ultimate compliment.

I'd offered to do a little proof-reading for him a time or two—just in the area of grammar because he tends to say things like "I'd ran," and "I seen" on occasion. But he would have none of it. I wouldn't have changed any meaning or his style. But he didn't trust me. And I guess he didn't need it anyway. People seem to prefer the real him.

Just a few years ago, I've started writing. It had nothing to do with the fact that my brother had done that. But I showed him a few things I'd written. He's seemed to like them. I don't remember ever hearing a compliment or much approval at all from my brother. He was always better at criticism. Now and then our mother would tell me something he said that showed he liked something I did. Such as when they came to Eugene to see me in Brigadoon, my award-winning performance. To me he said only, "It looked kind of silly when you got up on that stool and sat

199

there." That was the best he could do. Mom told me at the performance, he'd said, "She's good isn't she?"

He's ninety now. And I've gotten only approval from him for my writing. And he's also admitted he likes my potato salad. I'll settle for that. I think we've arrived.

THE U OF O
And My Friend Pegge

33

My mother and a friend of hers, Jack Tozier, drove me from Coquille out to Eugene when I entered college in September 1949. I wanted to major in music. A high school teacher told me I should go to the University of Oregon. So that's what I did.

I was the first, and only, in my family to go to college. My dad had gone only through 8th grade, and my mother had one year of high school. Their family situations precluded their finishing. And my brother went into the Army Air Corp just out of high school, the end of his formal schooling. So I had no background to give me a hint as to what college entailed.

It was exciting, driving out, but as the trip wore on, reality set in that I was going to be left there, and I felt like a child, a little afraid and homesick. I didn't altogether like the idea of staying. After all I was only 18. And I'd spent few nights away from home prior to this.

But we said goodbye, and I faced my future at Rebec House and the audacity of matriculating at the prestigious University of Oregon. I soon started looking forward—enthusiastically.

Rebec House sat where the old Sacred Heart Hospital

now sits, on 13th Avenue in Eugene, right across from the Dairy Queen, which went in that year. Rebec was an old, brown, 2-story, somewhat barny house with a big porch across the front, a large entryway with stairs leading to the second floor where most of our rooms were, a big living room to the left, and behind that a dining room big enough to seat 30 girls at meals. Behind that the kitchen and assorted other rooms. I'd never been in a house of that size before, and to me it seemed grand though I think some thought it should have been torn down.

I was greeted by the housemother, and a few girls were milling about, getting settled for the new school year. I was shown to my room, the bathroom (yes, singular, but with two showers and two stalls) and the screened-in sleeping porch with 3-tiered cots where we all slept. I met my three roommates, I brought my stuff in and settled down for a four-year stint.

Pegge was one of my roommates, and the one I got to know the best. She was a sophomore that year and taught me all the rules. About closing hours, and study hours, and that you were supposed to use them to study. I think she thought I might not make it without some prodding.

I did okay gradewise that first year. Straight As or nearly so. Kind of like high school. They make it easy on you the first year. Pegge seemed both pleased and surprised.

She also told me about many of the campus rules. Like closing hours. For girls only. The boys could do anything they wanted to. Stay out all night or whatever. But our doors locked at ten every night and a little later on

Saturdays. And it was a serious infraction if you got locked out. Also you couldn't wear any type of pants on campus. Jeans, slacks, or pedal pushers. Skirts only.

The only hope for that was if you rolled the pants up high enough that no one could see them, under a full length, buttoned up coat, you might get away with it. But it was serious if they caught you. I never actually heard what they would do to you. Expulsion? I don't know. Some of us did that one Saturday, and didn't get caught luckily. It's the only rule I ever intentionally broke. And I still don't think it hurt anybody.

When I was a senior, one girl in our house was 25. She had returned to finish school. She might have been married for a time. Two weeks before graduation she erred in staying out all night, probably thinking no one would notice. But the house mother must have. She was expelled and not allowed to graduate.

I also heard about two sisters who were in a sorority. It was probably the sorority rules which objected to girls dating a person of another race. Each of them dated an African American, and they were kicked out of their sorority. They might have been allowed to stay in school. I'm not sure.

We weren't all that uncivilized. We were stunned that that would happen. I resented the closing hours, and the dress codes. I think most of us did. Not because we particularly wanted to stay out late. It just seemed unduly rigid. And just for girls. We didn't do anything about it. No demonstrations. But I still resent it. We needed an ERA back then.

Pegge was also a social promoter and arranged outings for several of us girls with a bunch of boys, friends of her boyfriend, Richard Scofield.

Mel was among that group. Pegge and Richard later married, Ruth and Ted married, and Mel became my first and only real boyfriend. He graduated and was drafted into the Army and the Korean war, I graduated two years later and taught for three years. And then I married Mel Bishop, the best thing I ever did. I would never have met him if I hadn't met Pegge.

Thanks, Peg.

TRUE CRIME

34

Coquille is 18 miles over a curvy 2-lane road from Bandon by the Sea, and the only thing between us and the Pacific Ocean is the little coast range that sometimes lets the fog roll over and settle in the valley.

That is the way it was on the Friday night that Ruth and I were driving home from work at 11 PM from our swing shift at Georgia Pacific at the edge of Coquille where we stacked battery separators on our job that summer.

Ruth, one of our roommates in our first year at the UO, in '49/'50, came home with me as we planned to get jobs there. My cousin Bette was working with us as well, after graduating high school. So we were three girls, 17 and 18.

Ruth stayed with my mother, my grandmother, and me at our house 3 miles from town on a dark country road with nothing but a few houses here and there along the way. Bette stayed with her sister and brother-in-law about a quarter mile further down the road. My brother Boyd and his wife and child lived in the quarters built on at the back of our old service station, now unused, which sat out by the road, a few yards from Mom's house, which was to the side and farther back.

Boyd worked graveyard shift at the mill, and drove an

old Model A Ford to work. He left it in the mill parking lot for us to drive home when we got off at 11, just after he arrived. He arranged to ride home with somebody else in the mornings, and we three got a ride to work with somebody else who worked our shift, each afternoon. When we got home we parked the Model A under the overhang at the front of the service station.

Sixty-four years later, I cannot account for how Bette got home from our place, down the road to her sister's. I can't imagine that we didn't take her on home each night, but I also can't remember that we did, for reasons that may become clear from what I do remember distinctly. And Bette is no help because she can't remember anything either at this stage.)

The three of us girls rode home together every night except Fridays because Bette's boyfriend came up from Pistol River in Curry County for the weekends and picked her up after work on those nights.

Though Ruth didn't have a driver's license, she knew how to drive, so she did the driving. The Model A went frontward and backward, and I think that's about it. It didn't have many amenities, like a working horn, and its top speed was pretty slow. But Boyd liked his vintage cars. And there was little or no traffic on the roads late at night around there. Just an occasional car going to or from work.

One Monday, another dark and foggy night, Ruth and I started telling Bette as we started home, about what had happened the Friday before. We described to Bette how, just after we got on the road from the mill, and we approached a wide spot on the right, we saw a big, white car parked there, identified by Ruth, because I didn't know one car from another, as a Packard.

"It's coming up just ahead," we said as we neared the spot, and we continued the story that just as we had gotten to it, we saw a man in a suit and fedora, illuminated in the car as he lit a cigarette. It looked sinister. Why would a man be dressed like that in this area at this time of night? There was no night life in Coquille nor Myrtle Point, and he looked incongruous. He had simultaneously started the car as he lit the cigarette, and pulled out in front of us. Instead of stopping, Ruth whipped out around him, quick acting for driving a vehicle that barely goes. Now in front of him, we weren't sure if that was the best place to be.

At that point in the story, on this Monday, we approached the very spot we were describing, and to add more melodrama I said, "And there he is now!" as a big white specter materialized, looming out of the fog, and I recognized another white car parked right where the Packard had been.

Ruth said, "That's it!"

It was the white Packard!

I had just been kidding, not taking the whole thing too seriously, and trying to make a better story out of it.

He fell in behind us again, we gulped, and told Bette the rest of the story.

On the straight-a-way the Friday before, I had suggested that we slow down substantially so maybe he would pass us. Ruth had slowed to 5 miles an hour, but he stayed behind us the whole way, and when we pulled in at the service station, he pulled up outside the separation where the pumps had been, leaned across, opened his window, and, said coolly, "Hey, buddy, got a cigarette?"

Ruth lowered her low voice even more and gave him a gruff, "No!"

Apparently that was all that was needed. He said and did nothing more, except slowly drive on, proceeding down the road toward Myrtle Point.

What might he have done with two of us? Did he think he could handle us both at once? Or—?

But here we were with the same guy following us again. His persistence was unsettling, to say the least. He had obviously been watching us, and knew just where and when to wait for us. Now he knew where we lived. Who knew what his plans might be? He'd had a weekend to figure out how he was going to do whatever it was he planned to do. And he didn't seem to be at all put off by the prospect of having to handle two, or even three of us. So what was it? He was up to no good.

We drove slowly again to see if he would pass us. No luck. Again, he stayed right on our tail at 5 miles an hour in his high-powered vehicle.

What could we do to throw him off? It wouldn't make sense to stop at our usual parking spot at the service station. And we didn't want him to see us going into Mom's house. My grandmother and Mom were there alone when we were gone, and when Mom was at work, often on night shifts at the hospital, Grandma was there completely alone. Of course we had no phone. One of Mom's idiosyncrasies.

Maybe we could go on down to Susan and Don's house where Bette was staying. He wouldn't expect that.

Bette said, "Yes, Don has a gun, and we can call the police from there!" They had a phone. That seemed like a plan.

So we decided to just keep going, as fast as possible, considering the limitations of our vehicle, to throw the guy off and surprise him when we suddenly turned off. Bette and I would alert Ruth when to make the quick left turn onto Glen Aiken Road, because it was new to her, hoping he couldn't react fast enough to follow us. This was a little risky as there was a sheer drop off on the right side of the road we were turning onto, plus everything was pitch black and dense with fog. At least if he tried to follow us, maybe he would go over the edge, solving some problems for us.

There was a ludicrous side about a big fancy white Packard, with a grown man all dressed up in his suit and hat, in probably the only Packard in all of Coos County, following an old beat up Model A Ford in the middle of the night, with three mill-worker girls. What kind of moron is this guy?

We decided when we arrived at the house, just after the turn, that Bette would run in the house and tell Don, and call the police while Ruth and I waited outside to see if the Packard, heaven forbid, returned.

It worked. Ruth made the quick left turn without going over the drop off and the Packard didn't have time to follow us, so he proceeded on up the road. But just as we made the turn, Bette said, "Oh, I forgot! Don and Susan aren't home. They're out of town!" So there she was, having to stay alone at that house where this guy had seen us go. As I recall, she didn't seem to mind. I know I invited her to come back to Mom's with us. But she decided to stay. She would lock the doors. The house was old, all weathered wood and rickety. I'm sure if anybody really wanted to get in, they wouldn't have had much trouble. But at least she could call the police if needed. She went on in and called them while Ruth and I waited and watched outside.

The Packard didn't reappear, but after a few minutes, 2 police cars and 3 officers showed up, probably about three quarters of the Coquille police force.

We told them the whole story. Two of them drove on to Myrtle Point to see if they could spot the car. It was just another 6 miles, so it didn't take long to make the round trip. They said they'd found a white Packard parked in front of the hotel. It looked like sales materials and products in the car, and the car was warm, so it was probably the one. But just in case, while we left Bette there with two of the officers, one of them hunkered down in the back seat of the Model A, which was missing a horn and a few other essentials, while our unlicensed driver drove us back up the road to Mom's house. If the guy should somehow appear, he said, "Don't worry. If he tries anything, I'll plug him right in the gut!"

They don't have much action in Coquille.

We hadn't heard of Barney Fife yet in those days. But when we did, we recognized him.

We did appreciate those policemen though. They made us feel a little safer.

We got to Mom's house and waited around outside with our protector for a while. The guy wasn't there. After a few minutes the other two cops followed us up in their cars. Before they left they told us that when we drove home the next few nights, they would be parked along the road here and there, and we could watch for them. They would be as concealed as possible up in the trees, and ready for action.

Ruth and I went on into Mom's house, I'm sure locking the door behind us with one of those little skeleton keys you could buy in most hardware stores that would open or lock about any door that you might want to open or lock. That's all we had for either door.

We went into Mom's room, turned on the lights, and woke her up to tell her the story and about all the excitement.

After a while, in the dark on the back side of the house, we saw through her bedroom windows, a moving gleam of light illuminating the trees and shrubs, glancing ominously against the window frames. I had never seen lights behind the house at any time after dark. It looked as though it might be car lights. A gravel road went down the hill at the side of Mom's house, and her little detached garage entered from it. It appeared that a car had turned into the driveway of the garage and was maybe turning around.

Ruth and I ran to the living room to look out the front windows toward the roads.

A big white car moved slowly up the hill and turned right onto the main road, driving, as if reluctantly, past the house and toward Myrtle Point again. There was no way to report this now, so we went to bed and slept, but I'm not sure how.

We saw the police cars stationed along the road the next

couple of nights as we drove home.

We never saw the white Packard again.

Mom told her brother, Uncle Cince, a business man in Coquille, and he talked to the police about the situation. A few weeks later the police informed him that a man with a white Packard, similar MO, and general description was arrested in Washington State. I don't know what for. But he had a record as a sexual predator. They believed him to be the man we encountered, and that we had narrowly escaped.

I wonder if they were sure. It occurred to me only much later that they could have gotten the license number of the car in Myrtle Point and the name of the man registered at the hotel. I wonder if they did. At least they followed through with other jurisdictions. It is interesting to speculate about what he was capable of and how he would have handled 2 or 3 of us at once if he had acted on his obviously violent intentions.

We'd had a narrow escape. But we'll never know how narrow, nor exactly what it was that we escaped.

GRADES AREN'T EVERYTHING

35

It was one of two classes I flunked in college. I've always said—at least since the concept was introduced to me about 20 years later when I was studying counseling—that grades are pretty much meaningless.

It isn't normal to get straight A's because nobody is good at everything. If you get straight A's, it means you're working more for grades than for learning. Even the most highly intelligent, diligent student is weak or lacking deep interest in some areas.

But the strange thing is that I was deeply interested in these two classes, and I learned a lot. They were among my most memorable.

Dr. Edmond Cycler was a large, distinguished music professor in the string department, who handled himself with great dignity. I couldn't believe it when I learned that he had been an elementary school teacher at Riverton, a tiny community a few miles down the Coquille River from where I grew up, and I've heard that he was originally from someplace in the Midwest. I thought he must have been from some exotic place like Germany, or Belgium.

He taught Music History, and I entered the class without any former exposure to the subject. The first orchestra I ever heard in person was when I was nearly grown.

Dr. Cycler was a great speaker with his deep baritone voice, and his lectures held my interest. He spoke mostly about music's different historical periods, from Plainsong, Baroque and Rococo through Classical, Romantic, Impressionistic, to Expressionistic, the last of which occurred at the turn of the 20th Century. And he tied it's evolution in with all the other arts, painting, sculpture, architecture, and writing. I'd never known they evolved at all, let alone concurrently. It was a world of information, explaining so much and giving me a whole new way to appreciate the arts.

Then he gave a test.

It didn't have a question on it about anything he'd talked about in class. We'd had no textbook. I hadn't known we were supposed to get that information, or where. I think everybody else must have had some background. At least I don't think any of them flatly flunked.

Anyway he let me go on to the next class. This time we were each assigned to study a composer and give a report to the class with a performance of one of his pieces. I had an obscure composer for harpsichord, whose name I don't remember, from the Baroque period with its little flourishes and embellishments, and I played it on the piano. I don't remember what kind of a grade I got that time. But I passed. Maybe he thought since I'd suffered through him twice, he'd just give me the benefit of the doubt. But anyway, I was totally fascinated, and he was a fountain of learning for me.

The other class was sociology. Similarly it was one of

my most interesting subjects. And it broadened my outlook on the world. Coming from a provincial little town in Oregon, I had a lot of broadening to do.

One thing he talked about was the power of religious leaders and how church ministering is one of the easiest pursuits to get into an influential, respected category as a leader in the community, along with the true professionals.

I'd never thought of that. But I recognized what he was talking about. I'd had a distant cousin from Arkansas who became a preacher with almost no education. He performed in a fire and brimstone style which kept your attention. He was entertaining, and at least you didn't fall asleep in church when he was preaching. I liked him. But I don't think he measured up to other well-educated professionals, nor was he a particularly good model for the community. He later took up with a woman other than his wife, which didn't speak well for him and his religious zealotry.

This sociology professor gave objective tests, multiple choice and true or false questions. The statements were long, convoluted explanations that usually had a word in them that made me question their total accuracy. I was suspicious. I knew the answers; I just didn't know if his wording was a trick. So I flunked.

I told him I'd learned a lot, and wanted to take the class again, but that his questions seemed ambiguous. Why doesn't he give essay tests? He let me into some other of his classes, and after that, surprisingly, he gave essay tests. I don't know if it was because I suggested it. But I got A's from then on. Probably because I was able to bluff my way through those.

I was talking to a housemate the following year, who had the same teacher, and I mentioned one of his tests that I'd particularly enjoyed. It was to compare Communication and Socialization. I got carried away and filled up a Blue Book. She told me she knew about that. He'd told them about it and read my writing to the class! That was fun to hear.

I never got any direct feedback from him other than the credit for the class because it was a final, and I never saw him again. So I don't know if he actually liked my writing, or if he read it as an example of what not to do. But if that was it, she was polite enough not to tell me.

And I prefer it that way.

ME AND ATHLETICS

36

Sports have never been at the top of my list of avid interests, though when I pay attention they can be fun.

But in college, '49 to '53, I often went to football games, long before Autzen Stadium was even a gleam in someone's eye. Being a person who prefers a spur of the moment lifestyle, I rather yearn for those days when at noon at Rebec House, we would start talking about whether we wanted to go to the game or not, would decide by 12:30, walk over to Hayward Field, buy tickets, and be sitting in the stands for the kickoff at one. Of course there were only 4000 regular students in those days. Actually I think we rarely missed a game. I now can't remember the names of the stars, but we had some. I do remember Jim Loscotoff, later a Boston Celtic, and Bob Peterson of basketball fame. We also attended most of those games.

While I did and do admire those athletes, I also enjoyed some of the accoutrements of the games. The only yell I remember was the one we used when playing Oregon State College, which was not yet a University. It went, "Black and Orange, Black and Orange, Black and Orange," then singing down a musical 5th, a long, "B———O———" That might tell you something about the level of sophistication at the more advanced U of O than the Aggie school north of us.

In 1952, my senior year I somehow got on a committee to pick a theme for a homecoming parade float. Several sorority girls, one male, probably a frat boy, and I met at one of the sororities to brainstorm some ideas.

I knew nothing about sororities except that when we had occasional exchange dinners, they served things like artichokes. Luckily my Arkansas-born-and-raised, farm-wife-with-7-children grandmother had taught me how to approach an artichoke, dipping the leaves in butter. Several of the Rebec girls didn't have that advantage and weren't sure how to proceed. I don't know if they had fingerbowls or towelettes, but I wouldn't be surprised. We were more down to earth at the co-ops.

We met at one of the sororities to pick out a float theme. There was no brainstorming whatsoever because no one could think of a thing, even the guy, our leader. After about an hour, he said, "Well, I guess we'll just have to do something else," and he started to gather his stuff and leave. At which time I, who had been harboring what I was afraid they would think was a lame idea, screwed up my nerve, and ventured, "How about having a Duck musical director with a baton, and a Cougar dancing to his direction, and we could call the float 'Dance Our Ditty, Kitty,' using one of the Duck songs for the music."

Since there was no other idea of any kind, he thought it might work, and went away with that one.

That is exactly what they did, and it won third place in the float competition. Yes, there were more than 3 floats in the parade—a lot more. Not so bad. I never got credit for that of course. That guy probably claimed the idea for himself. I didn't expect any recognition for it; I didn't expect a plaque. But I did notice that nobody even mentioned it to me. The guy probably didn't even remember who cooked up that idea. My one contribution to athletics at the U of O, or anywhere else except when we were forced to take PE in high school, and once I served a volleyball and made a basket.

The world has so much to offer. Athletics isn't the only thing I've basically missed. I could name many things I should have appreciated more. Sooner.

THEATER LEGEND SPURS WALK DOWN
MEMORY LANE

**(This story printed in Write On for the
Register-Guard in 2003)**

37

A naive, stage-struck, 18-year-old freshman at the University of Oregon in 1949, I felt so fortunate to have entered college in the very term that the new modern world-class University Theatre had its grand opening! So I put on my formal and high heels and struck out alone, in the dark, from Rebec House up 13th Avenue past the Lemon O, the Side Inn and Taylor's and sashayed across campus on that November evening to watch "Winterset"— as I recall.

That is all I remember about the play, if even that is correct. But I definitely remember the thrill and historic significance of that moment. If I felt it at all, I managed to ignore the fact that I didn't fit at this grand occasion. I now know that those in attendance were mostly university patrons or Eugene socialites.

I had never heard of Horace Robinson, so didn't know he was responsible for the theater's existence.

Later that year I ran into Robinson when I tried out for "The Girl I Left Behind Me." I was ignored after the first reading, but since I hung around at the break, he invited me to read again. Never having worked with a real director, I had no idea how to take direction, and after several evenings of readings couldn't sustain the lengthy ha ha ha guffaw laugh that he required, so I didn't get the part.

Two years later, I signed up for Robinson's Technique of Acting class which turned out to be my favorite class of all time. After two terms, he asked me not to continue for the third term. I leave it to your imagination to speculate why. I didn't ask.

Not to be denied, without apology, I signed up anyway and showed up. To his credit, it was never mentioned again, and he gave me all the time and attention that I needed. He even complimented me a couple of times, which happened so rarely for anyone that I was the subject of some generous "Wows!" from others in the class. Behind his sometimes gruff exterior, Robinson is a kind man.

I never knew what to call him. He just wasn't a Mr. Robinson, and I never heard anybody call him that. Others called him Horace, and I think he was comfortable with that, but I wasn't. It seemed presumptuous to me, so I didn't call him anything to his face. If I wanted his attention, I said, "Uh—" and stated my case.

After participating in small ways in several plays, I tried out again for a real part the next year in the University Theatre musical, "Brigadoon." This time I got the part and even, to his credit, and a little bit to mine, won the coveted University Theatre award for Best Supporting Actress that year, hopefully redeeming myself a little bit in his eyes.

See, this is kind of a Cinderella story.

That was in 1953.

Obviously, I didn't make a career out of theater. But I'm in good company. Most stage-struck people don't make careers out of acting. If they did it would be like turning on more neon lights in town, dimming the sparkle of the real stars overhead. So, actually, failure can be a contribution!

Instead I wisely got married and had four kids, among many other endeavors, including participating in some amateur theater activities through the years.

In October 1999, I noticed that Robinson himself was performing at the now renamed Robinson Theatre with some of the members of a reading group that he has been conducting for years.

I had my son drop me off, and didn't realize until I got there that the performance was the kick-off for the 50th anniversary celebration of the opening of the University Theatre! This was in the month of Robinson's 90th birthday and was an amazingly entertaining and nostalgic evening for me. To see Robinson still going, filling in the dots for me between the past and the present on that stage that I had run all over and commanded for a minute! Oh, the smell of the greasepaint and the roar of the crowd!

In that de ja vu moment, I decided not to call my son as planned for a ride home. It seemed ordained. I should walk. So I gave my head a dramatic toss and set off alone in the dark — in the other direction this time — across campus to my home of 28 years, marveling at the coincidence of it all, contemplating my good fortune for having crossed paths with the best director in the world, and wondering where half a century had just gone.

The air felt the same. I could smell William's Bakery, just like always. For a minute I thought about sashaying, but I walked, a little slower this time, and this time I was wearing tennis shoes.

AN EDUCATION IN PASADENA

38

In 1955 when I was 23, I saw an ad in a theatrical magazine for an "Actor's Showcase" at Pasadena Playhouse. I had just finished my second year of teaching after four years of college where I spent a fair amount of time at the University Theatre in classes and productions. In addition I had been entertaining for years through high school and college, and I was teaching speech and drama and directing plays and shows in Myrtle Point High School.

This sounded like a good last fling, another theatrical experience, and who knows, maybe a career in the movies! So I signed up, paid the tuition, and drove to Pasadena. I was directed to my room where I met my roommate and settled in. As it turned out, I was the only one with a car. Everyone else had flown in I think. So anyplace we needed a car for, I usually had mine full.

One day a group of us drove out. As I pulled into traffic, we found we were in a procession of some kind. So we just joined the parade for a while, and nobody objected apparently. It turned out to be with The King of Siam. I hadn't expected him to be there. I guess he had time to travel as his country had become Thailand by then. Imagine that. Me and the king in the same parade, me in my blue '51 Ford. A memorable once-in-a-lifetime experience once we knew who it was we were honoring.

The attendees in the Showcase numbered around fifty I imagine. It included about an equal number of young men and women from around the country, all aspiring to be "discovered" like Lana Turner at Schwab's drug store as the story goes.

Only one, a younger and relatively-pretty red-headed girl, with no discernible acting talent, seemed to attract any attention along those lines. I think the Playhouse project was disappointing as nobody showed up who met their standards.

Everyone in the group was congenial and mutually supportive. A couple made suggestions to me about learning to speak Standard English. I had a few speech idiosyncrasies from my Southern family background such as saying "about" and around like "abaaout" or "araaound", turning them into almost 3-syllable words with a deep gully in the middle, chewing my words like some do in Arkansas, emphasizing final r's instead of dropping them as they do in the deeper South. That was one of the main things I learned in Pasadena. Even though I've never totally put it into practice, as evidenced by the number of people who still ask me if I'm from the South, and by what I hear when my voice is recorded. I did a real estate ad once for radio, and I've recorded on my answering machine, which always surprises me when I hear myself.

We enjoyed many experiences around the perimeter of

225

Hollywood culture.

Several of us visited a hair salon, I included, where I had an updated cut. It was the famous fifties "ducktail".

A photographer in the neighborhood, known for filming the stars, attracted several of us to patronize him for glamor shots. One of mine, he blew up and featured in his window. That was fun. It was a seductive-looking pose of me, seated, leaning forward, holding a long cigarette holder. He had added a whiff of smoke wafting up from the cigarette.

A couple of our group members had found a pizza place they urged us to go to, explaining how you eat it. "You roll it up from the pointed end, and then eat it with your fingers." That's what people were doing all right. But I've never seen that done since. Of course it was years before I saw another pizza. That seems strange now that there is a pizza place on every block in the country. You have to be pretty old to remember when there wasn't.

A trip to downtown Hollywood one evening treated us to a sighting of the famous, black-curly-haired Jeff Chandler out for a stroll on a deserted street, except for us and the woman he was with. It surprised us that she was dressed simply in a white flared skirt and white shoes, looking a little dowdy You would expect a glamorous sophisticated type to be with him. When they saw us, they turned into the entrance of a closed hardware store and stood with their backs to us looking into the window full of tools, obviously trying to avoid us. Surely they weren't interested in staring at a bunch of tools for 10 minutes. A younger boy among us walked over and stood right beside Jeff, shoulder to shoulder. No one said a word or acknowledged each other's presence, except for one or two of us saying, "Come on, Chas," which didn't hurry him up. It was clear that the star wanted no attention. But the kid got a thrill I guess. And something to tell when he got home. After an interminable period, he gave up and we walked on, as did Jeff Chandler and his partner, unmolested but clearly uncomfortable.

We had instruction in dance, and acting in movies, for which we had to discard everything we'd ever known about acting. It is necessary on stage to make everything broader than in real life because you are a distance from the audience and must project your voice to the last row of seats, even if it's a whisper, and your gestures must be larger than in real life in order to appear normal to the audience.

But in Hollywood it's another story. There's no upstage and downstage to be concerned about, and you do everything small. The camera can zoom in on the smallest movement, so you would look crazy gesturing broadly or projecting your voice as if you were a block away.

We did some scenes in the classes and had a final performance with some kind of an audience—not a filmed performance, but on a stage, though acting as if we were in a film, in a muted, subdued style that had no perceptible impact on the audience.

Then we put on a variety show that anyone who wanted to, could be in. I sang "Boston Beguine" from "New Faces of 1952" The piano accompanist wasn't up to the task. I'd had a wonderful accompanist at the U of O where I did that song several times, and who backed me up perfectly. I heard no comment, good or bad from any instructor we had, for me or anyone else, about anything for the whole summer. But one member of our group was generously complimentary to me on my performance. It was a red-haired guy named Marty Ingels who was constantly funny, and kept us in stitches all the time. He was a great comedian who later became moderately well-known in TV and movies. But his fame had no connection with being "discovered" at this event. In 1977 he married Shirley Jones. His comment about that was, "When we got married, Shirley got presents from all over the world, and I got 19 letters of disbelief and two death threats."

Marty Ingels is the only name I remember of anyone in the group.

One day someone heard that Twentieth Century Fox was holding tryouts for "Oklahoma". So three of us went down. Why not? It turned out they were trying only dancers that night so I just stood around and watched. The other two tried out. One of them showed evidence of having had some familiarity with dance. The other one looked about like I would have. When we left they gave us each a check for $3, which said "Twentieth Century Fox" on it. I thought about framing mine. But spent it instead. It's just as well because I wouldn't be able to find it now anyway. Fox produced the movie, and it was fun to watch, having seen some of the preliminaries. And of course Shirley Jones got the lead.

A big party was held at the playhouse, and several of us stood on a balcony, looking down at the stars who came in, Marlon Brando, and Angela Lansbury, among others.

Throughout the summer, from time to time, we would run into familiar faces from the silver screen as we rode the elevator or walked through the halls

Toward the end they brought in a speaker for us. David Susskind. What I remember of that, was his message for the females among us, that if our teeth weren't fixed or if we had any physical variations from the perfect standard, get fixed. And if we were past 19, we were over the hill, past our prime, so don't bother. Several of us in our early 20s looked at each other and left that summer, satisfied that we'd given it a shot—at something we didn't know that we wanted to be a part of in the first place.

It was a memorable summer, mingling with the stars, more or less, learning about pizza, parading with the King of Siam, and learning what it was really like out there in the glamorous world of Hollywood. But little else.

Back home, I became engaged to marry Mel Bishop the following year. Before going to bed one night, Mom said "I'm going to take your picture down to the Sentinel office tomorrow for your engagement announcement, so put the one you want in the paper, on top of the stack by the phone, so I know which one to use." The next morning I was awakened by a burst of laughter from my mother, at the other end of the house, and I knew she'd found the picture on top. It was the demure one with the cigarette holder. I can't find that one now either; it's apparently gone the way of my check from Twentieth Century Fox.

NEW TEACHER

39

My first year of teaching, in 1953/54, was in Lorane, a little farming community 20 miles southwest of Eugene.

The high school had 40 students and four teachers. I taught mixed chorus, English Classes, and a social studies unit that I had to write myself. Also I went to the elementary school a couple of times a week to teach general music.

As the music teacher, I was also expected to play piano for the local Christian church on Sundays. I'd done a lot of that so it was no problem for me. But looking back—

I still had friends from the U of O in Eugene, so often drove over on Saturdays to see them. The only problem was, the road to Lorane wasn't paved, but covered with shale, which cut up your tires. I had 14 flats that year, sometimes on that trip back after dark on Saturday nights. Usually somebody came by and stopped to help. I think I changed the tire one time myself.

The next two years I taught at Myrtle Point High School, with mixed chorus, English classes, and a speech and drama class. The drama class put on a couple of variety shows for assemblies, and I directed the junior and senior plays, doing all our practicing after school

The principal called me to his office. He had something to tell me.

"Just in case you should hear this somewhere later, I wanted to explain to you—so you wouldn't misunderstand. We have another new teacher this year, just beginning. But he will be paid a bit more than you—because he's a man, and of course will have a family to take care of eventually, and just needs more, you know. I just wanted you to know that so you wouldn't misunderstand."

"Oh, of course," I answered. Actually I felt really grateful to have just been hired.

Nevertheless, that was one of my most satisfying teaching jobs. They were supportive and expressed appreciation for my efforts. The principal said about one of my variety shows, "That was the best production we've ever had here." That made up for my meager pay checks that I never gave any thought to anyway.

At the end of 1956, Mel and I were married and I moved to Seattle with him. Up there I got a job at Eckstein Jr Hi in a high end area in northeast Seattle. I was hired as a full-time substitute for a teacher who was away on sabbatical for a year. And I was paid about half of what a regular full-time teacher was. I learned from some teachers later that there was no teacher on sabbatical that I was substituting for. They said others have worked for substitute pay too. One man, they said, had been doing that for 14 years. That was a little disillusioning for a place like Seattle.

There I taught all general music and one eighth grade

English class. A girl told me at the end of that, that she had finally learned some grammar, so she could understand it. That was nice to hear.

The principal called me to his office twice that year. Once because I'd let a kid teach the class how to commit a certain crime. He said, "Did you have a boy give a speech to the class on how to hot wire a car?"

"Yes, it was for a unit on making speeches, and I asked them to explain to the class how to do something they were good at."

"And you actually let him stand there and make a speech about that?"

"Yes, I thought it was a healthy interest. I've known a lot of boys who like auto mechanics."

"Well, we've got some parents who are pretty concerned about it."

"I lost my keys one time when I was teaching in Myrtle Point, Oregon, and some of the boys hotwired my car so I could get home. I found that really helpful, and didn't know it wasn't okay to do."

"Well, we can't have students talking about how to steal cars."

"I'm sorry. I'm from a small town. That's my only excuse, I guess. And I never knew of any car thefts. It's different here."

I think he was appalled, and I don't know for sure that he accepted my answers. But it was a fact. I've never pretended to be that sophisticated.

In one of my music classes there, I was telling the kids about the famed classical pianist, Arthur Rubenstein, and

232

an eight-grade girl said "Oh, I met him once, at a party my parents gave." They also told me about trips they'd taken to faraway places, places I couldn't imagine. They were way ahead of me.

The other time the principal called me in, was late in the year. He said, "We know that you are going to have a baby, and that you won't be coming back next year, but we haven't gotten a notice from you about that. Of course you will be staying home and taking care of your baby next year."

"I don't know," I said. I did plan to stay home. But I didn't want him deciding it for me. That was the way it was left. Maybe he was just using that as a way to put me out without saying "You're fired."

The end of my teaching career for the next fourteen years when I became a hausfrau and stayed at home with my four kids.

THE WONDER OF HAVING KIDS

40

It's natural for most people to want children—a way to be significant in the world. Mel said it's how you create eternal life for yourself; the way you live on is through your kids.

We knew we wanted to have some eventually. Fortunately nature took over, and the first one was born on Aug 23, 1957. So we brought a baby home to celebrate, two days later, on our first anniversary.

Everybody who mentioned it, was sure it would be a boy. I was basically awkward and plain, and I think I remember hearing "tomboy" occasionally. Do they think only pretty little things can have girls? But I fooled them. I had an adorable baby girl, doing a huge amount for my self-esteem.

I tried to be the perfect mother. I started reading to Christy at six months. That was one thing I did right. When she was 18 months old, I opened the ABC book we'd been reading, and she said "D" when she saw it. So I checked and found out she could name them all. She could read all the capital letters anywhere she saw them such as in her dad's New Yorker magazines.

I thought if she can read the letters, she could read words, so I started printing short words. She soon had a reading vocabulary of 40 words such as toy, boy, girl, book, story, play. I got some easy little books, and she was reading them shortly after turning two. I know, many little children memorize books and sound as if they are reading stories they have heard repeatedly, but she really was reading— new stuff too. She learned by sight, no phonics, and grew up to be the fastest reader I've ever known outside of her dad who also never knew phonics. Christy says she doesn't remember learning to read, feeling as though she always could.

She didn't say much except just single words until she was two. We were outside as Mel was getting ready to drive downtown for some errands. She put her first words together and said, "Bye, Daddy." Mel just melted.

While still two, one day she was sitting on the floor, struggling to get her Stride Rites on her wide feet, and I had to listen closely to hear what she was saying. "God damn shoe." That wasn't part of my vocabulary. Her dad wasn't quite as discerning though. Another day when I was struggling to get them on her, she suggested, "Say damn, Mama, say damn."

In later years, I commented that my kids were fairly quiet. Her brother, Littlejohn said, "But Christy makes up for the rest of us." A bubbling personality.

When she was three, in Germany, I was baby-sitting for a couple's two-year-old and an infant in our third-floor apartment while they went on vacation. Our second was two also, so I had three in diapers and three on bottles, and was quite harried by the end of the two weeks. Neither of mine were climbers, but their's was, I found out. I heard

Christy scream frantically for me, and I ran to the kitchen where I found the 2-year-old on the window ledge, leaning out of the window I had left open, and Christy hanging on to his clothes for dear life. I'm sure she saved him as he was struggling to get out the window. I decided the parents didn't need to know that story. They got their children back, each in one piece. Thanks to Christy.

In kindergarten her class was putting on a Christmas program. One of the girls who had a long part, didn't show up. The teachers didn't know what to do. Christy was sitting on the floor of the stage with her feet straight out in front of her in her black tights and corduroy jumper over a white shirt, looking like a big doll. (Even a couple of other mothers said so. "Who is that adorable little girl sitting there? She is sooo cute!") I had to admit she was mine.

After hearing some of the discussion about how to handle the missing part, Christy volunteered matter-of-factly, "I can do it."

"Do you know the part?" one teacher asked.

"Yes."

They were doubtful, but eventually decided it was their only option so proceeded to start the program. Christy did the whole thing perfectly as if she'd had the part from the beginning, astounding the teachers. Christy thought little of it. She's lived most of her life that way, solving problems as they arise.

After one month of first grade, we took her out of school for a trip through Europe since we were going back to the states in December, thinking the trip would be more important than staying in school. Her wonderful teacher,

236

Miss Ojima, wrote out assignments for her to do while she was away, and made her a little book to write stories in about things she saw on the trip. She wrote about and illustrated the Leaning Tower of Pisa, Michelangelo's statue of David, including the fig leaf, or lack of, and the windmills in Holland. She returned to school only briefly after we returned and before we left for the US.

Back on US soil, Christy started her second full month of first grade in January. They started trying to teach her phonics, and she came home trying to sound out some words. Rose came out "rah-suh". I told the teacher, "It is just confusing her. She can already read "miscellaneous" so she doesn't need phonics." So the poor teacher figured out something else to do with her.

Christy was always sensitive to other people's feelings and developed early a strong sense of justice. When she was eight, in the third grade, she came home with her eyes on fire. A group of kids were picking on another one, calling him fat, and bullying in general. She got between the boy and the group and told them they'd have to fight her before they got to him, to get out of there and leave him alone! I can just see her with her hands on her hips, daring them to try anything more. They backed off.

That must have meant a lot to that little boy. He had a kidney disease which made him look distended and heavy, and sadly, he died just shortly after that.

Christy was a good start for having kids. We couldn't have been more pleased. My self-esteem went way up, and her gift to me has been immeasurable.

LITTLEJOHN

41

Every child is full of surprises, and sometimes it never seems to end. You don't know who you're going to get, you don't know what they'll do, or where they'll go.

Our second birth they thought might result in twins, but it turned out to be just one extra-big one. He was a couple weeks late coming into the world, was 23 inches long and weighed in at 10 pounds 7 ounces.

If it was a boy we would name him John Melvin after his two grandfathers. When Mel saw him and was told his size, he dubbed him Littlejohn as in the big friend of Robin Hood. It stuck.

After having a pretty normal baby girl who cried a fair amount and kept us up at night as they usually do, this one was a breeze. At birth they didn't make him cry. They just laid him on a table across the room for a while, worrying me a little. But he lay there looking around as if trying to figure out what to make of it. The doctor said he looked and acted like a 3-month-old. He held his head up from the beginning. The first night at home he woke up once and whimpered slightly, was fed, and went back to sleep. After that he slept all night and ate 3 times a day. If we wanted to see him, we had to go wake him up. We didn't hear him cry until he was six months old when he was sick with a sore throat.

Due to the sore throat, we couldn't fly with the baby, so our move to Germany was postponed for a month to October when he was seven months old and weighed a healthy 27 pounds.

We did a lot of traveling during the four years we were there. The last trip included an audience with the new Pope, Paul VI, at the Vatican when Littlejohn was 4. There were hordes of people. We were at the front when He was carried through. Suddenly I was alarmed and said, "Where is Littlejohn?" He was missing. A man next to us said, "One of the guards took him over to see the Pope." He had picked up Littlejohn and run with him so the Pope could touch him. And then he returned him to us. He'd been blessed. Too bad we weren't Catholic.

By that time we'd added Scott, followed by Todd later in Washington, DC. The boys were blond and like stair steps. Occasionally somebody would offer to take one of them. Mel said, "Nope, we can't break up the set."

Littlejohn was always easygoing and seemed to handle every situation with ease. At six he started playing drums in "The Patriots", a drum and bugle corps. They wore three-cornered George Washington hats and played in parades. He continued to play drums in school from then on, and single-mindedly pursued the art.

On his 12th birthday, we were having dinner, at home, and he said to us, "Thanks for bornin' me." We were touched at that thoughtfulness. Then we started talking about what they wanted to be when they grew up. Littlejohn said, "A Garbage Man". I laughed, stupidly. Mel said, "There's nothing wrong with that. It's an important job, and we need good ones." He was right of course. We were always proud of our kids. They've done nothing not to be proud of. And much to be proud of. And we'd have been proud if Littljohn had gone on to be a garbage man.

The honors and recognition he has had for his accomplishments and vast contributions to the music world though would have meant so much to Mel the jazz lover as it has to me.

GERMANY, HERE WE COME!

42

I'd always wanted to see the world. Getting acquainted with Seattle was probably as much as I could have hoped for after growing up in the Oregon country around small towns. But, as I've said, I married well.

We lived in Seattle for the first three years, had two children, and moved once. That had kept us awake nights. The first place was a one-bedroom duplex on Queen Anne Hill where we lived for two years, but we decided we needed two bedrooms with the second one on the way. We were paying $65 a month rent, and would be going to 75. Could we manage it? After a few sleepless nights, in Seattle, we threw caution to the wind and moved.

We didn't know anybody who'd been to Europe except for the war. But I was getting seasoned.

After about a year in our new housing, Mel came home one day and announced, "We're transferring to Germany! What do you think?" What did I think? "Yeaaay!"

We started packing. We parked our stylish garage sale furniture, the baby's bassinet and crib, and other assorted items with a couple who agreed to keep them for us. Of course we lost touch over the years, and never came back to

Seattle, an ill-thought-out idea in the first place that we would come back to reclaim our stuff someday. But I was fond of the art deco couch, and would have liked to have kept the bassinet for posterity.

We took along the little wooden table and chairs that Mel had put together and painted, only one chair with two rungs backwards that gave it a little awkward tilt, an occasional table he made out of a door with legs attached, and the piece of driftwood with the empty wine bottle for decoration. We also took all the books and records. Heavy stuff. Our personal belongings and clothes of course. Fortunately the government paid for the move, with limitations. The movers said we weighed in just under the wire. Lucky us.

In 1959 air travel was still sparse. Planes weren't required to have radar to detect other aircraft until '55. Before that pilots just had to make eye contact to avoid other planes in the vicinity. "In 1950 there were 950 aircraft in the skies, multiplying to 1647 in 1959," the internet says.

"The first nonstop commercial flights across the U S happened in '53, and the first true transatlantic liner was Pan American in '57." So things were still primitive in '59 when we left. I don't know what kind of a plane we took to McGuire Air Force Base near Trenton, New Jersey, but I'm sure it wasn't nonstop. I should have kept a diary.

Once there, we had to stay on base, on alert, until 10 PM in case there was a flight available. We were excited to be so close to New York City. It seemed a shame to miss it. So the first night at ten, we bundled up the kids and set out for New York. Christy had turned two a couple of months before, and Littlejohn was seven months old. With his 27 pounds, and Christy a little more, we had two hefty loads to tote around. Two big healthy kids.

We took a 90-minute bus ride to downtown New York, and walked up and down a good bit of Broadway spotting famous theaters and other sights, marveling at the number of yellow cabs, the streets looking like broken egg yolks running together, with a ratio of maybe one civilian car to 50 cabs.

We might have set a record if anybody had noticed. I suspect we were the only couple who ever made that trek in the middle of the night with two kids slung over their shoulders and a diaper bag and two blankets dangling. A friendly New Yorker, rare we'd been told, helped us get to a subway where we took a ride. An eerie experience, with one strange-looking man the only other passenger, and the silence, like moving through the catacombs, setting the stage for wondering if this was such a good idea. But we made it back, and we could say we'd been to New York City!

Without much sleep, we had to be up early the next morning, packed and ready to go on a moment's notice. Sometime that day a plane was available. We were ready for the transatlantic flight, on a military prop plane, and sat down in the waiting room, well-named we found, because we waited, and we waited, and waited—while they fixed the plane. For hours, before we were finally told we could now board. Relieved, we lined up.

An official appeared at the door, and made an

announcement. "No, not just yet. They aren't quite ready. There's a little problem with the plane. But they're getting it fixed. You might as well go back and sit down." So we all trooped back to wait some more. There we were with two babies and all the gear we had to carry for them, to last 'til we got to the other side of the world, a diaper bag, bottles, baby food, toys, books, extra clothing, and a couple of blankets.

After another hour or two, we boarded and were on our way. Well, that is, after sitting on the plane another hour while they made sure. We hoped.

The hostesses on these military planes were heavy-footed WACs who clunked up and down the aisles, grim-faced. I had a feeling they didn't like their jobs. A GI across the aisle pulled the life jacket out of its pocket in front of him, and was looking it over when one of the WACs strode by, jerked it out of his hand and put it back where it belonged, without a word and without missing a step. As she disappeared down the aisle, he said, sort of to himself, "Just trying to read the directions. I'd look pretty funny bobbin' up and down in the ocean trying to read the directions."

We were on our way to Greenland! To refuel I suppose. It was dark so we couldn't see a thing. I could only imagine an arctic panorama of ice and snow. But I've been to Greenland! Then off to Germany. After a few hours, we made an unscheduled stop in the Azores. They had to do a little adjustment on the engine. We felt confident they knew what they were doing.

I didn't even know where the Azores were. I would

have guessed in the South Pacific, but they must be somewhere in the middle of the Atlantic unless we were really off course. Geography was never my forte. It was the middle of the night, and pitch black so we could see nothing there either. But I imagined an exotic environment, and enjoyed the surprise of being able to say I've been in the Azores!

We boarded again, and headed for Germany.

Christy had just gotten potty trained, so wasn't wearing diapers. The restrooms on the plane were totally scary. I couldn't reassure her that she wouldn't fall in, though of course I was holding and trying to encourage her. She managed to have no accident on the flights though she never used the facilities for the whole trip.

We'd been up, that is, out of bed and awake for 35 hours by the time we landed on German soil, which I noted when I stepped off the plane, looked exactly like ours. I don't know what I expected German soil to look like. Like Germany I guess. The way I'd expected California to look like California on our first trip there when I was eight.

Mel's new boss met our plane in Frankfurt, and drove us about an hour and a half to Kaiserslautern, where we would be living and working for the next four years.

Mel rode in front. I sat in back with the babies, enjoying the scenery. I said, "What is that I see up on the hill on the left?" It was a brick structure of some sort. Could it be? "Oh, that's just an old castle." An old medieval castle! My first! I thought of the fairy tales I grew up on. Knights and Ladies, Kings and Princesses. It was thrilling! So this is Germany!

When we got to our temporary housing, an apartment on the fourth floor of a walk-up at the American hospital in Landstuhl a few miles from Kaiserslautern. The boss's wife and another couple of co-workers were there getting the place spruced up and equipped for us. A high chair by the table, and two cribs in one bedroom. They left a casserole still warm in the oven.

What a beautiful, friendly welcome. They said goodnight and left.

We were home.

GERMANY 1959 - 1963

43

As we acclimated to Germany, we recognized two distinct aspects.

Everything seemed dark, the buildings, bare of paint, in shades of brown and gray, occasional rubble and concrete bunkers that the Nazis had hidden out in. The women looked dowdy in heavy tweed coats. Some of this we brought to it with our awareness of the horror of the place—Hitler, and the SS.

At the same time, they enjoy Christmas with jollity, color and lights. Most of the towns and cities seemed to have Christmas bazaars or festivals unmatched anywhere I've been. We'd arrived not long before Christmas 1959, so got to enjoy four of them.

The war had ended just 14 years before so we walked among people who had lived there during the Hitler era and the war. They were still suffering the effects and some poverty. Most of the locals we knew lived in tiny apartments, no bigger than one or two small American bedrooms, which worked only by placing all the furniture touching arm to arm, and visitors sitting knee to knee with the hosts.

I rode a city bus a time or two, and saw some customs new to me. If you were on a bus at ten AM, you would see big hausfraus pull out long sausages or hams from their bags, big knives, and loaves of black bread to make hefty sandwiches as they rode along to their destinations. They sawed back and forth on the bread, and sawed off some meat to put together for their mid-morning snacks, and passed them out to their children. I'm sure they all ate their continental bread and coffee breakfasts, and then a meal again at noon so even I, the bottomless pit, couldn't see how they could take in such a humungous snack at ten. The first time I saw this, I mentioned it to one of my American neighbors and she laughed and said, "Oh yes, it's their mid-morning snack." She'd seen it too.

Mel's office in Civilian Personnel for the Dept. of the Army, in Kaiserslautern, was in one of the kasernes, which I learned were German army barracks.

We lived at Vogelweh, a housing development for American military officers and civilian employees, about four miles west of Kaiserslautern. This is the largest American community outside of the U. S., which probably accounted for my inability to learn the language because most of the Germans in that area spoke English better than I did.

About six miles beyond that, Landstuhl, the county seat, with about 9,000 residents, nestled between two high peaks. The American hospital sat on one, at the west side of town, opened in 1953, now the largest American hospital in the world outside of the U S. Mel hired personnel for them as well as for the schools, and other civilians serving the military. We lived in housing there for our first six months in Germany. Across from that on the east side, the other peak held the ruins of a looming medieval castle, built in the 1550s by Franz von Sickingen, the Sickingen Schloss.

We enjoyed Landstuhl and frequented the Stadtkeller (City cellar) a restaurant in a basement which served things like wild boar stew, cooked with dried fruits, and a little cup of what seemed to be lard, to use as a spread much as we would use butter. A bare taste was more than enough of that. The decor was ancient armor, shields, and other remnants of the past. There we were fascinated by how the *herr* always entered first, followed by the *frau* as he pulled back the heavy brown velvet curtain that covered the entrance, and then proceeded to nod and greet everyone in the place—*"Guten abend, guten abend"*— before they sat down.

Another restaurant that we liked was the Gruen Lanterne which served more common German fare, weiner schnitzels, wursts, and more.

Living in Germany at that time afforded us many interesting experiences that relatively few Americans could enjoy in those days. At the bottom of the hill where you turned to drive up to the hospital a little *kirche* stands, with a cemetery in the yard, which we were informed (to put everything in perspective for us Americans) was built and has been functioning since before Columbus discovered America. Of course we saw many truly ancient Roman ruins after that. But the *kirche* was a start for us.

Germans dote on their children. They have charming toy stores with dolls as cute as their toddlers, and the famous Steiff toys. All the youngsters seemed to be on the streets bundled up in snow suits during the winter, and they were adorable children. However they never took them to restaurants. We took ours out to eat, and they made every effort to accommodate us though they didn't have high chairs nor special children's menus as we were used to at home. But they welcomed us and doted on our children.

On warm days around Easter, they displayed boiled, colored eggs on stands outside in the sun, where they seemed to sit for several days until they were all sold. Some of the Americans looked askance at this. I didn't buy them. They dismissed us with a wave, "Oh, you Americans."

The country held more of interest than you could take advantage of in four years. Bavaria was colorful with painted and timbered chalets, the Alps, and the "Mad King's" castles built in about 1880. Ludwig II, King of Bavaria from the age of 19, a close friend of Richard Wagner, and with probably a sad side to his eccentric and isolated life, built the popular and magnificent "fairy tale castle", Neuschwanstein high on a mountain, and the elaborate Linderhoff, glowing white, full of swan décor, gilt and glitter, with white swans on its lake and a huge fountain, spouting high into the air.

We visited Garmisch and Berchtesgaden and stayed at the Eibsee Hotel, which was a Hitler retreat, but had now been taken over by the American military and its employees, so we took advantage of it a couple of times. It had dark wood, marble, and huge bathtubs, bigger than any I've ever seen in the US, but similar in size to the ones in our apartments over there. The porcelain sinks were outsized as well, and each room had a balcony where you could walk out and look over Lake Eibsee. But we couldn't throw the awareness that we were walking and sleeping where Hitler had been at home just a few years before.

This was near the foot of the Zugspitze, the highest mountain in Germany, where Mel and I went to ski one time, my first time on skis. The only way to the top was on a tram, or a train. It was a steep ride that took half an hour or so. We could see who were the blasé regulars because they dozed, paying little attention to the scenery or the ride except once when the train jerked to a stop, and they woke up fast and looked alarmed, exclaiming to each other. "What's happening?" What's happening?" (Or whatever Germans say—it sounded like a few swear words) which undermined our confidence because it obviously wasn't a common occurrence. And we wondered if their brakes would hold or if we would go flying backwards down to where we started. But they recovered and continued up.

Mel and I were wearing our new ski sweaters, but most of the men skiers were bare to the waist and the women in bra tops. The air was light and warm at that altitude. We didn't exert ourselves too much, just played around on the little slopes on top of the mountain. No steep slopes for us. I don't remember falling down. Imagine that. But we displayed ourselves as a couple of those weird or ignorant Americans bundled up in our new sweaters.

Other travels included magnificent cathedrals and walled towns such as Rothenburg and Nuremburg, and other medieval castles. All going back to ancient times.

We visited Dachau, a small town south of us at the edge

251

if Bavaria. It had the concentration camp nearest to us, probably the smallest of all of them. The railroad tracks running up the main street of town to the camp was an eye opener. The German people didn't know? That's what they all said. They could NOT have not known. The box cars crammed with people again and again, the smoke stack towering at the edge of town. Where did they think those people were after they'd been brought there? And certainly it could not have been hidden from the whole country. I met one Dutch girl who said, "Of course they knew. We knew. They certainly did." I suppose it would be like Americans saying they didn't know about the lynchings in our country that have been so rampant, or that they don't know about people of color being judged differently than others. We all know.

I read now, on line, that "people were gassed at some of the other concentration camps but not at Dachau." But the first room we were taken into was the "baths" where people were directed to remove their clothing and go in for a shower. We looked up to see the "shower heads" which they told us had then emitted deadly gases to kill the whole room full, who clamored to get to air. The bodies would be found in huge piles. Then they were carted to the ovens. We saw those too. And the piles of ash outside the buildings, still there after 15 years since the end of the war. I wonder how large they were before the rains and winds started on them. They've apparently cleaned up the place and the reports about it since we saw it. I doubt that the piles of ashes still exist 50-plus years later. But there were certainly enough to last for 15 years, and many more I'm sure. We signed the visitor's book before we left. One person had written, "God Damn filthy Nazis".

But Germans love Christmas. And they have lovely traditions. Beautiful ornaments available everywhere, street festivals in every town with booths for food and gifts, people eating bratwursts in hard buns with hot mustard, carnivals with rides for little children, carousels and calliopes. All music, color and bright lights.

My daughter Christy and I flew back a few years ago. She was six when we left. She is now in her fifties, and she remembered much from our life there. We were surprised. Houses are painted in nice colors now, much like in France, with blue, green, yellow, and pink. The people are stylish. Everything seems happier.

We also visited some places we couldn't before. Eastern Germany, because of the wall that went up while we lived there. We saw Bach's church in Leipzig, still running, in which he is entombed, his house across the square and the Bach museum. Unbelievable and thrilling. And we saw Mendelssohn's house and his friends', the Robert and Clara Schumann's, home, just a few blocks away. Other beautiful and amazing cities such as Dresden, which had been rebuilt after the war an exact replica of the original with the rubble recovered and used to rebuild.

Back in western Germany, after some search, we found the courthouse where the Nuremburg trials were held, another reminder of the tragic horror of that time and place. They even let us go into the courtroom where a trial was going on. It's been in use for all these years, and looks like an ordinary courtroom. It wasn't easy to locate. We almost expected to see signs directing tourists to the building. They did have pictures that lined the walls of the hall outside the courtroom, of the famous trial and the evil men who were tried there. But no other mention of it.

It makes you wonder what could happen in other countries. Could the United States turn fascist? In Germany they elected Hitler after he had clearly described his intentions, which he carried out. Did they really get what they wanted?

THROUGH THE BRITISH ISLES

44

Our first vacation was three weeks in October 1960, and I sang my way through most of the United Kingdom. (Or thought my way through some songs. Mel would have balked at listening to me for the whole trip.)

The first time was when I stood alone on the deck of the ferry as we approached Dover. The cliffs really are white, and I was viewing them under a clear blue sky at dawn. A beautiful and unbelievable sight. I couldn't deny myself.

"There'll be bluebirds over the white cliffs of Dover, tomorrow, just you wait and see——. There'll be love and laughter and peace ever after, tomorrow when the world is free——." I wonder how many times the captain had heard that.

It was still early for most of the travelers apparently. Mel was suffering from seasickness after the ride across the rough English Channel, and felt he couldn't leave his bunk. So I found myself alone on deck, and at liberty to belt out that song as I snapped pictures of the thrilling view.

We had driven about 365 miles from Kaiserslautern to Calais, on the Northern coast of France, the day before, and caught the ferry to Dover. They gave us booths for the all-night ride even though the Dover strait is just a few miles across. I've since read that they move much slower than daytime trips, to avoid collisions with other vessels that would be hard to see in the dark, and to save fuel. At the time I had not realized it was such a short distance as we'd tossed and turned and rolled for hours. Some sites say 46 miles. Others say it's about a 20 mile trip.

Mel managed to get up after we reached port. We retrieved our car and drove into Dover, a quaint little town out of the distant past, where we walked on the narrow cobblestone streets among the timbered cottages, as if we'd been transplanted into another time. One of the houses had a restaurant sign, so we stopped in for one of the famous English breakfasts. It started with porridge, cream and sugar, followed by plates of eggs, an assortment of grilled meats, a grilled tomato slice, and warm rolls just brought in from a nearby bakery. Butter, marmalade, and tea to top it off. The reason I'm able to remember the menu so well is that it was the same all over England. And, of course, I'm food-oriented. Amazingly Mel was able to handle this repast, seemingly fully recovered from the English Channel malady.

The drive north through England afforded us picturesque sights of thatched roofs and Tudor architecture, reminding me of my English ancestry, the Stones and Watts, my father's line, and the Beckhams, my maternal grandmother's.

We made a stop at Stonehenge, and saw ancient castles straight out of story books.

At that point we were heading for Scotland. I pictured

clans, plaids, kilts, and bagpipes. And when we got there, I wasn't disappointed. We also saw the Finley name, my maternal grandfather. Had I known at the time that Macbeth ("Yes, the Macbeth!" they said on Ancestry.com) shows up in the Finley ancestral line, we would have tried to find his castle. Inverness castle I understand. Or maybe we even saw it, but it didn't hold the significance it would have if I'd known.

I think that's spectacular. Even if he was not the most admirable of men, he is a historical figure that Shakespeare found interesting enough to write a play about.

He lived from 1005 to 1057, and was King of Scotland for 14 years. Some of his offspring were kings too. I suspect the population was pretty sparse then. It was probably like being the king of a small town now.

We drove straight to Edinburgh, and in the search for our reserved bed and breakfast, stopped at an intersection with several exits, mulling over which one to take. A townsperson strode over to us. "Can I help ye," he asked with a big smile. Mel told him the name of the street we needed. He clapped Mel on the shoulder, and gave him an enthusiastic push with every accented syllable, while gesturing broadly with the other hand. "Aye! Ye go oop the hill and arrroond the bend, and ye canna miss it! Welcome to Edinbourrrough!" We thanked him profusely before we got far enough away to allow ourselves to erupt in laughter. Was he a plant? Put there to entertain tourists?

Son Todd had a similar experience 53 years later. On Facebook he told how he hadn't been in Scotland for 15 minutes before he was hearing "oop and doon", the F-word with a long U, and "Ye". He felt like he was in a movie.

We loved Scotland. I had just been in the musical, Brigadoon, at the U of O seven years before, and had to learn the brogue. It is a beautiful show about an imaginary village in Scotland which comes to life every 100 years.

I wanted to burst into "The Heather on the Hill," "There But For You Go I," "My Mother's Weddin' Day," or "From This Day On," but—I just couldn't pass up, "Brigadoon, Brigadoon, in thy valley, there'll be love——"

I felt like I'd just landed in Brigadoon. Or in some fairyland.

Our hostess in the old brownstone house with the tall double doors, where we stayed, fed us the breakfast, but additionally, she sliced up a more-than- generous plate for each of us, of "sausage" that "joost came in from the highlands, And I want ye to have some," she enunciated enthusiastically.

I knew what we were eating, and we tried to ingest a respectable amount to be polite. I could see from the expression on Mel's face that he knew what it was too. But neither of us mentioned it until we were away. It tasted much like, and had a similar texture to liverwurst. We'd never had that for breakfast either. But this was, of course, blood sausage.

There were other food specialties that we didn't try, such as the national food, haggis, which is "offal and innards" cooked up with vegetables and oats in a sheep's stomach, and served with Scotch. An American recipe for haggis says, "You can serve it with mashed potatoes, if you serve it at all."

258

One Sunday evening, we were out and decided it was time for dinner. We stopped at an obviously open restaurant and told them we wanted dinner. They said, "No, we aren't serving dinner." So we tried a couple of other places with the same results. Finally at about the fourth place, "We said, "Well, is there any place that you know of where we can get some food?" "Oh, yes, we have High Tea. That includes food." We accepted that. We had to wait while he went to check and see if there was a table. There was. It was a huge room with maybe two tables in use, and 50 empty ones. So he ushered us to one of them, back some place in about the middle, and we had a great meal while being entertained by some strange combination of string players and a drum set.

In Scotland they had no locks on the doors at most or all of the bed and breakfasts we stayed in. Reminiscent of home in Oregon during my childhood. In all the countries, they brought bed warmers, pottery stones that held hot water, and tucked them between the sheets in the evening before bedtime so we didn't completely freeze to death. Some invited us down to the main room where we could huddle around the little electric heater, which they turned on in the evenings.

We hadn't had electric heaters at home when I was little, but otherwise much of what we saw in Europe, reminded us of 30 years earlier in the US. We used rubber hot water bottles to keep our feet warm at night, and we had little central heating and few cars.

Breakfasts in Scotland and England were often served family style with all the lodgers together at one table, most of them English. We found them always to be outgoing and friendly, kind of surprising, as America's view, (or at least ours) of the English is that they are quite reserved and proper. But Americans are the ones who more often tend to speak quietly, or you might say secretively, around strangers and in public.

Driving down the west coast of Scotland, through the fields edged with stone walls, we saw a peaceful scene of sheep and cows backed by the Atlantic Ocean. In the early morning there was a little stone cottage and a milk maid in costume walking with her bucket toward the barn. Another perfect stage setting. A blue and white scenario to be remembered forever.

We made a quick trip to Ireland, storing our car overnight, and renting one on the other side for a day's drive around. I was in *Finian's Rainbow* at the U of O several years before, and it brought to mind "How are things in Glocomorra? Is that little brook still leapin' there? Does the laddie with the twinklin' eye, come whistlin' by? And does he go away, sad and dreamy there, not to see me there?"

Staying in Dublin overnight, we attended a play at the famous national Abbey Theatre, by some major playwright of yore, whose name I can no longer remember, maybe because it was the longest and most boring production either of us had ever seen. It might have been by Sean O'Casey.

But that was all right. Once while there, I was certain I caught sight of a leprechaun straight out of Finian's Rainbow. He was green anyway. I could almost hear him,

"When I'm not near the girl I love, I love the girl I'm near."

We also saw the Blarney Stone which, if you kiss it, supposedly gives you eloquence forever after. My memory has faded, and I don't know if I kissed it. But I doubt that I would have kissed a rock that everybody else and his brother had kissed. It doesn't sound exactly sanitary. But I could have used the help with the eloquence. Too bad.

Back in Scotland, we looked for the monster in Loch Ness. No luck. We took each other's picture in front of Loch Lomond, mine as I was belting out, "Oh, ye'll tak the high road, and I'll tak the low road, and I'll get to Scotland afore ye. But me and my true love will never meet again on the bonnie, bonnie banks of Loch Lomond."

And that in fact, was true.

Somewhere along the way, we drove through part of Wales, where the signs were undecipherable with their strange language. We stopped once though so Mel could take my picture by a sign that said "Maidenhead". He couldn't resist, either because it was the only sign we could read, or for some other reason.

Back in England, we drove through the smokestacks of Liverpool, picturing Oliver Twist, and visited more castles along the way. Then we headed into London where we went to Trafalgar Square, Charing Cross, and Berkley Square. "That certain night, the night we met, there was magic abroad in the air. There were angels dining at the Ritz, And a nightingale sang in Berkeley Square. I may be right. I may be wrong. But I'm perfectly willing to swear—that when you turned and smiled at me, A nightingale sang in Berkeley Square."

We visited some little art shops, bought painted tiles that I use for trivets, some old leather-bound books for neighbors who asked us to find some, and we went to the Tate Gallery where we bought a print of a page from the Book of Kell which still hangs in my dining room. We stopped by a dark wood-lined pub for lunch, and Mel got to wondering if I should be there because there were no other women. However nothing was said, so we stayed. We went to Westminster Abbey and the Tower of London, where the Crown Jewels are on display. We ate fish and chips, and saw the Tower Bridge.

"London Bridge is falling down," and "Ring around the Rosie," came to mind. Went by 10 Downing Street, the Prime Minister's residence, and watched a changing of the guard at Buckingham Palace.

In Scotland, we had bought a white wool sweater for me, a Harris Tweed jacket for Mel, and a tam for him and each of the kids, among other trinkets and memorabilia. The sweater was well-worn by the end of the trip because the weather, though sunny and clear, was freezing cold, and I never got bundled up sufficiently to be comfortable. I decided I would just have to suffer through it, and wait to get home and let it all sink in.

On the way home, we drove part of the way through France, and stopped in some small town, at a little hotel where we could have a meal and get some sleep for whatever was left of the night. We parked in a well-lit area right in front of the hotel door, so we just locked the car and left all the stuff except a couple of suitcases in it rather than try to unload for such a short time.

In the morning, we found that somebody had broken in and taken the two fluffy, warm comforters that my mother had made, Mel's new Harris Tweed jacket, and a pair of shoes. That was all the major things. Most of the rest was still there.

It was a bit of a slap in the face for the end of our eventful trip. But they couldn't steal our experiences and memories, and we still had a few mementos left. Part of another song came to mind. "You can't take that away from me—"

But now we were eager to get home to the babies. And the first thing I planned to do was sing them "London Bridge" and "Ring Around the Rosie."

STONEHENGE IN OCTOBER

45

It was a dark and stormy night. Well, not really stormy. Actually the weather, while icy cold, was beautiful, clear and sunny with blue skies for our whole three-week October trip though the British Isles. We'd gotten baby sitters for the kids back in our government housing in Germany. Christy was three by now, and Littlejohn was one and a half, and we thought they would be better off at home, even without us, than dragged around the continent. Tonight provided proof that we were right about that.

We'd been in England for a couple of days by now, and neared Salisbury as this evening wore on, a few miles from Stonehenge on our drive north. Mel suggested maybe we should just find Stonehenge, park there, and sleep in the car so we could get up early and see it in the daylight before driving on. It sounded like a good idea to me. It would save us a few pounds—the cost of a B&B for one night, and in a few hours we'd be on our way again. At this time there were no tickets required to see Stonehenge, and you could walk freely between the stones, in and around, no parking fees, and no fences.

The car was our '59 Volvo, which we had bought new

just a year before when we arrived in Germany. It was a small, white sedan, and one of its nicer amenities was that you could fold down the backs of the seats and turn them into beds. We'd never done that yet, but tonight we would initiate that side benefit and save time and money, rolled up in a couple of thick comforters that my mother had made and we'd brought along for just such an occasion. So Mel started that operation, which required you to use a wrench to remove some bolts which held the seats together.

We were parked right in front of this famous landmark. Stonehenge! There was no way for me to help so I just wandered around looking at those big ancient stones, silhouetted tall and black against the night sky. I knew little about Stonehenge except that they've stood there since 2000 or 3000 BC! It is hard to believe. Even much of the Roman Forum has crumbled and fallen. But these tons of stones were placed so they have never wobbled in all these centuries. It seems like a superhuman task to get them there and set them up that securely. Nobody knows exactly who it was, and how or why they did it.

There they stood. Stark. Out in the middle of a moor that looked like outer space with no end. A cow wandered by, and I saw one in the distance. Everything was silent. There was nothing else, not even a building in sight of this place. Only a couple of deciduous trees stood nearby.

I walked back over to the car. Mel was still working at getting it apart. "I didn't know it would be so complicated," I said, "I didn't know you'd have to take it apart."

"Neither did I," he said and went on working at it.

I wandered away again, to gaze around.

265

A wind came up, and I began to hear dry leaves rustling, breaking the silence as they were whipped around and skittered across the parking area. Then silence. Another gust with skittering leaves. "Who built this place?" I thought, "The Druids?" I began to imagine I was seeing them in their flowing black robes, moving among these giant pillars doing whatever Druids do. I think they were sacrificial pagans. Is this a burial ground? We're going to be sleeping in a cemetery. I wonder how these people died.

Where did that wind come from? Like a Druid spirit's breath blowing the leaves. Trying to tell us something?

I walked back over toward the car. "I don't know if I can sleep out here," I said, "This is getting spooky. Listen to those leaves blowing." I think Mel agreed with me though reluctant to admit it. He'd gotten the seats apart finally. It had taken quite a while. A bigger job than you would have expected. I was ready to pull out of there. But you couldn't drive the car that way. I don't know what you'd do if there were an emergency. And this felt kind of like one to me.

"I'll try to get it back together," he said and started working on reversing what he'd just done. We were completely alone out there.

Auto mechanics was not Mel's forte. So I just hoped he'd be able to get it back in working order. There was nothing to do but stick it out. So I gazed out again at that expansive moor with those stones looming over it. All we needed now was for a fog to roll in and for the Baskerville Hounds to come yelping through.

Mel seemed to be trying to hurry. I think he was almost

as spooked as I was. After all it was October, when pagan spirits get active. Years later, I hear they have decided this was a burial place. But that the Druids didn't have a part in constructing it. Doesn't matter who made it. Call them Druids, Gauls, Celts, or early Britons. Whoever they were, I caught glimpses of their shadows moving silently among the stones and across the moor—appearing, and disappearing just as fast, as I waited. And no, I don't drink.

We started wondering, "What if we couldn't get the car back together at all?" We'd just have to huddle locked in it all night and get no rest watching for apparitions to appear at the windows. And then worry in the morning about how to find somebody to get the car in condition to drive again.

But finally Mel accomplished the task, having used up a good bit of the night, and I gave a big sigh of relief as we climbed in and headed out to find the nearest B & B, secure from an October night on an English moor, rife with specters and ghosts. The only remnant I found of that experience was some black lint on my sleeve, which I couldn't account for.

I did manage to express appreciation for Mel's doing all that work on the car, signifying nothing. It had seemed like a good idea at the time.

Halloween 1960 had come and happily gone. It was the scariest one I'd experienced, and there weren't even any masked and costumed ghouls and goblins. No pretending, no tricks or treats. This was the real thing! And it wasn't even October 31st yet.

We would gladly return in the morning to see Stonehenge in the glory and safety of the welcome light of day.

The idea of sleeping in the car was never mentioned again.

COINCIDENTALLY——

46

Sometimes events defy the imagination.

While we lived in Germany, we were included in recreational and social activities of the military.

I had always been involved in amateur theater to some extent, fancying myself a thespian. A service club several miles away on another base, was bringing a show to our local service club.

It was Brigadoon, and I had to see it because I had been in that show at the U of O ten years earlier, a highlight of my college career. Our leads were double cast which gave us the opportunity to watch a dress rehearsal of our own show. So I know whereof I speak. Ours had been a tremendous production on a new, world-class stage. I couldn't imagine that this could be an adequate performance with no stage, no orchestra, just on the floor at one end of a little service club with a piano accompaniment. Frankly I expected to be feeling quite superior after watching this feeble attempt at such an ambitious undertaking—a full-fledged musical comedy in such a venue!

Was I ever surprised! The pianist was great. The acting was right up there, the music lively and beautiful, the direction professional. The girl who played "my part" actually did some business similar to what I had done, and she sang the songs faster, as I had done, than in any other production I'd seen including the lame traveling Broadway show. It was an entertaining and superior performance!

I had to go up and compliment them. I was just beginning to speak to "Meg" when a guy in costume said, "Jeanette!" and to her, "This is the one I've been telling you about!" (Well, now, how could I not think she was great?) He was the director as well as an actor in this show, and he had been in the crowd scenes in our production at Oregon a decade before. I hadn't actually known him so didn't recognize him in costume here. But clearly he had been very observant and turned out the best production I've seen outside of ours at Oregon with the great Horace Robinson as director!

What are the odds?

ANOTHER AMAZING OCCURENCE:

I was active in the drama group at that club and was chatting with one of the GIs in the group. He said he was from New York City. I tried to think if I knew anybody from there, and could think of only one person, out of the however many million who live there. So I said playfully, "Well, let's see. Do you know Ed Kenney?" He looked stunned.

"He was my roommate!"

270

"What? THE Ed Kenney?"

We ascertained that he was the same one. From Hawaii, he had been the wonderful tenor lead in Brigadoon at the UO and was in Flower Drum Song on Broadway.

AND ANOTHER:

And then again some things just seem to be preordained.

When Mel and I were married, we went on a honeymoon to California, and stopped by the redwoods on the way south. A guest book was sitting open on a stump, and Mel said, "Come here and write your name. This will be the first time you write your new name won't it," he said romantically.

I thought for a second or two, remembering, and said, "No, it will be the second". Unintentionally, maybe I deflated him a little.

My maiden name was Jeanette Stone. When I was about 12, I started thinking, overconfidently, one day, "Sometime I'll get married and change my name. I wonder what it will be." I say "overconfidently" because later I learned that it would almost require a miracle to find the right person who would also want to marry you. But in my naiveté I stood at my blackboard on the kitchen wall and started writing down some last names I'd heard, trying to pick out one I liked. None of them seemed to fit, so I erased them, and then wrote one more, including my first name, "Jeanette Bishop". The whole thing seemed silly. What would be the likelihood of my meeting somebody with that name who would want to marry me, and I him? Besides I didn't particularly like the name. So I erased it and thought nothing more of it.

Until that moment.

I related that little true story to Mel, leaving out the part about not particularly liking the name. He didn't respond, but stood looking puzzled. I couldn't tell if he didn't believe me, and I still don't know. I thought my story had a touch of romance or predestination to it. But whether he believed me or not, I think he was thinking, "I've married a crazy woman." And I wrote Jeanette Bishop for the second time.

AND ANOTHER:

Some things that happen don't seem to have any meaning, but they sure are fun.

After Germany we lived in Washington, DC, for about six years, and then moved with our four kids—daughter Christy, and sons John, Scott, and Todd, to San Antonio, Texas. We stayed in a motel for a couple of months waiting to find a house and close the sale, and were out by the pool one day, chatting with another couple in similar circumstances, who also had 3 little boys. Their names, they told us, were John, Scott, and Todd!

"What?"

After somewhat recovering from the surprise at that coincidence, I said, "Well, we also have a daughter." The woman said, "We don't have a daughter. But we have a dog. Her name is Christy."

She called the dog over to prove it. "Here, Christy." And here she came!

272

Then it turned out they had at one time also lived in Vogelweh, the housing development where we had lived iin Germany, in the building next to ours!

Truth is sometimes stranger than fiction.

OUR CHRISTMAS ANGEL

47

He was born on Dec. 13, 1962, just in time for Christmas. What do you do about a birthday for a person like Scott Bishop? Especially one who exhibits no greed, and who doesn't want presents or celebrations of his birth.

Born of American parents in a foreign land disqualifies him for being President. I told him this so he wouldn't harbor any aspirations along that line and be disappointed. (He thinks this isn't necessarily true. After all John McCain ran for president; somebody must think that it isn't. So who knows what might happen.)

Our third child made up for the first two, the first one in the medium range for keeping parents busy with her, the second one, so easy that we had to go wake him up to get to see him.

Scott, the third, was one of those who cried and screamed 23 and a half hours out of 24. I prayed for the three month period when most of them start sleeping through the night. I breathed a sigh when he slept maybe five hours straight one night. But then it was back to the usual, and we struggled to get half the rest we needed for his first year. We walked the floor with him, took him into bed with us, fed him again, sang to him, patted or rubbed his back. Everything we could think of to do. Even after the first year, he had "night terrors" when he couldn't be consoled. The doctor said he was gaining weight and growing properly. He didn't have an answer. I don't think Scott has ever slept well for a whole night.

But he grew to be a quiet, pleasant person, bright, funny, entertaining, and caring.

He had a hard time learning to talk. When he started trying, he couldn't make himself understood, and he seemed frustrated by it. At four I took him for speech therapy at the University of Maryland. He loved it. At first they thought he might be hard of hearing or slow. I knew that wasn't the case.

They made him books to add to for each sound as he learned to make them. The first one was the L sound. La la la, and they said to look for words that start with L. We saw a sign that said "Lobster" on the way home. And it went from there. After about four sessions, he was talking clearly, and he had learned more letters from the process, so he began to read. And that was the end of the speech problem.

He played with a little girl up the street whose mother told me Scott's friend said little prayers before meals. One day she listened closely as it sounded a little funny. She was saying, "Scott is great. Scott is good, and we thank him for our food."

Scott has never been greedy. We tried. He would open just one Christmas present, and it always took us several days to get him to open the rest while he happily created toys out of ordinary objects—like playing with the box. I always saw that he was highly creative. I'm right about that.

We landed back on US soil on his first birthday, living in Washington, D C, and later San Antonio where he started first grade. He was disappointed the first day because they didn't do any work, and seemed unhappy in school. We went in to talk to his teacher about that, and I took along a story he had written, with no help, about Abraham Lincoln, which was well-written and accurate. I thought it might be helpful for her to see what he could do. But she brushed it off as if totally disinterested. Only years later did he tell me that she had hit his hands with a ruler because he wasn't working hard enough. I wish I'd known then!

Scott and Todd had a room right next to ours in San Antonio. One night after we'd all gone to bed, Mel said, "Listen".

Seven-year-old Scott was softly telling his two-year-old brother the names of all the planets in order of their distance from the earth.

Our Christmas angel.

ITALY

48

It was different. Don't get me wrong. Italy is a country full of wonder, with its walled cities on hill tops, vineyards and villages that, driving through, you can smell the grapes (probably that they've stomped with bare feet for wine), their magnificent cathedrals, the Vatican with its Sistine Chapel, and all the remnants of ancient Roman history. Plus the people are colorful and fun.

But the minute we crossed the line, there it was. Litter. Paper and garbage strewn along the sides of the road. This was in October of 1962.

We had left Christy and Littlejohn with a sitter again, for our three-week trip. They were five and three, and we were sure Amelia would take good care of them. She came in one day a week and cleaned the whole apartment, did my ironing if there was any, polished the floor and watched the kids for a while so I could do some shopping. She even cleaned the refrigerator or anything else that needed doing. For $3 a day. That's what they charged. All the Americans had a German maid. Except me, until a friend was going back stateside, and asked me if I wanted her. (They took some ownerships in their maids, and could give them to somebody else if they wanted to.) It sounded like not a bad idea so I took her up on it. (A first for me, and for that matter, a last).

Scott was well on the way, obvious to anybody who saw me.

We stopped for gasoline soon after we crossed the border into Italy, and while Mel went inside, I got out to stretch my legs a bit. When here came a car whizzing by full of teenage boys. Yelling, laughing, waving at me. "Ooh, Hoo! Ooh Hoo!" I was just guessing. But I'm convinced it was in reference to my family way.

In hotels they quoted the price for a room. On our first night they said, 1,000 Lira. Then in the morning when we were ready to pay on the way out. 1,500 lira. Mel's inclination was to not argue the point, just pay it. Mine was to argue the point.

I said, "No. You said 1,000 lira."

They said, "1,400 lira."

I said, "No. 1,000."

They, "1,300."

I, "1,000."

They took the 1,000 lira with broad smiles, thanked us profusely, and wished us well as we left. They tried.

At one of the restaurants, the menu listed no prices. I asked for prices.

They said, "We'll tell you after you've eaten. Just tell us what you want." I didn't trust them. Mel convinced me it would probably be all right. It was. The prices seemed within a reasonable range.

Along the road we saw fruit stands with beautiful oranges displayed. Though I'd never really loved oranges like other kids I knew, I found myself craving some of those in my condition. Surprise. They were plastic. But they brought out a box of real ones. Little wrinkled dried out things that you would throw out at home.

Another opportunity arose for orange, in the form of juice at a restaurant where we'd stopped for breakfast. While they served continental breakfasts in Italy, they also offered orange juice here, at quite a high price. But we decided I needed some, so I ordered it. It came in a shot glass, with much of the juice displaced by an ice cube. So I got a taste is the best way to describe it. Mel left a tip on the table as we left. I picked it up as I followed him out. And I handed it back to him--of course.

Additionally, we ordered rolls and coffee at a given price, they bring them with butter and jam. Then the price went up substantially when it was time to pay. Again I confronted the price issue. They said "The extra is for the butter and jam."

"Well you brought it."

"You ate it."

They won.

Other restaurant experiences included a fly baked into my pizza in Naples. I was indignant, but when I called it to the waiter's attention, he just politely explained, with gestures and buzzing sound effects, that it had come out of the air. That helped. Then we more than once detected little worms in the leafy green salads they served. We'd been told never to eat raw vegetables such as salads in Germany because they used (I can barely say it.) human fertilizer on their crops.

But in Florence we ate in a great little restaurant which exhibited none of those idiosyncrasies. The food was delicious and clean, the walls had pictures of American celebrities, including Bing Crosby, who'd patronized them, Just ordinary prices. The best hotel accommodations we had were in Florence, with a square under our window with distinctively Italian music wafting up until late at night as we lay gazing up at our heavenly Rococo painted ceiling.

There we saw the Uffizi Gallery, full of famous paintings and sculptures by people such as Michelangelo and Rafael, and a square lined with sculptures all the way around, including a copy of Michelangelo's David, the original moved inside to protect him from the elements.

In Rome we visited the Vatican and went through the Sistine Chapel, envisioning Michelangelo painting the ceiling, lying on a scaffolding high above the floor. We took a guided tour around the city, which introduced you to the high spots that would take you days to cover on your own. This one included the ancient Colosseum and Roman Forum. Looking down onto the ancient marble ruins, one of our fellow Americans, in a loud Hawaiian shirt, commented to the guide, "It looks like they don't keep this place up very well." He sounded like one of those guys who would paint your shabby chic desk and ruin it.

The ugly American.

We climbed the Leaning Tower of Pisa, drove through Genoa, and on along the Mediterranean, up to Monaco and the pink palace, thinking of Prince Albert and The Country Girl.

On about October third In Milan we saw the first street

280

demonstration ever for us. People marching with signs that we made out to see that it was about the Cuban Missile Crisis, and it felt ominous. We also saw newspapers with the headlines.

Shortly before this trip, we'd taken a drive from Kaiserslautern on little back roads across France, as directed by the army for all the civilian personnel, so we'd be familiar with the escape route in case it became necessary. A poignant reminder that it wasn't that long since the war, and all the world's problems weren't settled yet. The Berlin wall had gone up by then. And now a problem with our ally the USSR.

If there were an evacuation while we were gone, what would happen to Christy and Littlejohn? Would somebody take them along? Could be ever find them again?

Mel convinced me that it wouldn't happen. So we finished the last few days of our trip, up through France where we stayed in a little room in Arles that looked exactly like Van Gogh's in his famous painting, and Switzerland where we ate in a lovely—clean—restaurant, and both suffered stomach upsets the next day.

We got home and found the kids, safe and sound. Except for when Amelia took them home with her, a strange place to them, and the kids were horrified to see her husband kill a rabbit. Not what we would have chosen for them.

VISITORS

49

The next year, October of 1963, we'd thought about Scandinavia for our annual trip. But then Mom came over at our invitation. She was there for several months, until we went back after our fourth year in Europe. We thought Mel's parents, Correen (Nanna) and Mel (Poppie) should be able to take advantage of the opportunity too. So they came for a shorter stay. None of them would have ever seen Europe on their own. We decided showing them around the central continent would make more sense.

Christy was six, and Littlejohn, four, so we took them along this time, but left 9-month-old Scott with baby sitters, an American couple.

We'd bought a Volkswagen bus for this trip, to hold all seven of us, and it wasn't a bad idea to revisit the same places. There's always more to see. We saw the new Pope in the Vatican where we literally fought the crowds. They're enthusiastic about the Pope, pushing and shoving their way to him. On the square, you couldn't stop. The crowd just moved you along. So we picked up the kids and carried them to keep them from being trampled.

Inside, we were in front where we could get a close look at the new Pope Paul VI as he was carried by. And this was when Littlejohn got blessed.

We also visited the Vatican souvenir shop where you could buy Blessings from the Pope. I got one for a couple of my Catholic friends. But they didn't act thrilled. And we bought a plainsong record. That was beautiful. But what I noticed was that among those records of sacred music, they had one by Little Richard.

In one city, it must have been Rome, we parallel-parked on a busy street, and just as Mel started to open his door, a bicycle ran into it, knocking the rider and his bike onto the street. He seemed okay, and got up. But a crowd formed immediately, and it turned out we were right in front of a police station. So they asked Mel to come inside. I wanted to go too, but Mel said no, for me to wait in the car. He was probably right. I could have gotten him imprisoned. The car door wasn't more than six inches open, so that bike was skimming along the sides of cars.

We watched the spectacle of people around us, all making that shaking gesture of the hand, that we've seen in the movies, with the palm up, the back of the hand toward their opponent. We couldn't help laughing. They really do that when they get excited about something. We couldn't tell whose side they were on, ours or the biker's. At the same time we were a little worried about Mel. Would they release him or imprison him? We'd heard of things like that. Foreigners being detained in a foreign country, innocent or guilty of some infraction.

But he handled it well, as I was sure he would, and they

were apparently reasonable, because after a time, he came walking back to the car, and we proceeded on to the rest of our trip.

We had come down through Austria, where we visited Mozart's place and saw his piano, on down to Italy, and then we drove up the west side through Genoa and out along the Mediterranean again, up through France, Arles, Van Gogh's town. Somehow we worked in Milan and up through Switzerland with its mountain that is so steep that the road constantly U-turns the whole way, to keep you somewhat horizontal instead of driving vertically straight up.

We took a separate trip to Holland where we stayed at the Visser Hotel as always. It was a small hotel, probably a private home originally, with steep ladder-like stairways, on a canal and about a block from the Anne Frank house, which we toured again. Mr. Visser and his wife ran the hotel. Somehow we learned that he would give us a tour around Amsterdam on request for no extra fee. We always requested, and he rode with us, patiently waiting for us at each site we visited. At a huge windmill, he climbed up a blade to the top for out entertainment.

I much later learned that Mr. Visser was Jewish and was a survivor of a German concentration camp during the war.

We enjoyed their breakfasts which were always the same, cooked and served by the two of them. Scrambled eggs, bread, butter, cheese (probably Gouda), and strawberry jam with coffee. Then we took him out on the town and, it occurred to us, left her to do all the cleaning from breakfasts and the rooms.

From there we made it home to Scott. He didn't seem excited to see us. He was okay. He was walking. We'd missed his first steps.

We took a few trips around Germany too while they were there, and eventually said goodbye to the Bishops. Mom stayed on until for another month and a half until we were ready to move to Washington, DC, where she would meet us. So we put her on a commercial plane to travel back alone. She couldn't ride on the plane with us. We would be going on a military prop plane again, a long, slow flight with several stops.

Mel explained to Mom to go to a certain hotel, which was near the Old Post Office Building in downtown Washington where he would be working. I'm not sure how he knew about it. We'd never been there. I believe it was called the Raleigh.

We flew in to McGuire Air Force Base in New Jersey, which we had gone over from. Then we boarded a train that took us down to DC. That was an experience. It was like something out of the past. Ornate, with its Redcaps, all black men, who polished your shoes, on your feet, before you disembarked.

When we got there, we discovered that the hotel that we'd directed Mom to, was closed. I couldn't quite imagine how we would ever find her. No cell phones then. We didn't have an address there, and I'm sure Mel had not provided her with any contact with the civilian personnel office.

There was another hotel.

We checked out the other hotel, nearby, somewhat similar to the Raleigh. Sure enough, she was there. Coincidentally, her taxi driver had suggested it to her when she gave him the other name. So we felt very, very lucky. Things just seem to work out sometimes. What would we have done if we hadn't found her there? I can think of no way we could have ever made contact. She enjoyed the stay and the food at their buffet restaurant with cooked greens, grits, and sweet potatoes.

So we found a motel room, moved Mom and ourselves over there, and started getting ready for Christmas, just two weeks away.

CHRISTMAS TREES I'VE KNOWN

50

The way I grew up, decorating Christmas trees was almost a moral issue. But I learned through the years that those rules aren't always adhered to and you might as well relax and broaden your mind on the subject in the interest of keeping peace.

I fondly remember the family trip each December out to the woods to cut a tree. It was a special event with a whole day dedicated to it. Daddy, with his logging background and ability to take care of anything, had no problem finding and cutting the perfect tree. We all tramped around through the woods, pointing out trees we thought might work until we agreed on one. That is, our dad, our mother, my brother, and I.

I don't think you could buy a tree then, at least in rural Oregon during the 30s and 40s. Tree farming hadn't developed yet. Wild trees in Oregon were still plentiful, but you had to go out and cut your own, and we wouldn't have had it any other way.

At home, the stand consisted of a bucket filled with gravel and water in which the tree was planted. Mom adorned it with a white sheet in lieu of snow, and after the lights, swags and ornaments were hung on, Daddy added the final touch by patiently hanging the hundreds of icicles, carefully, one by one. It was imperative that it be done that way, and it took a whole day to complete. It was perfect. We would all stand and gaze in awe and admiration at its glimmering beauty, and I ran to look at it the first thing each morning.

Years later after I was married, our marital bliss was threatened when we put up a tree and Mel started throwing icicles at it with abandon, from across the room. It turned out that is the way his dad did it, apparently thinking it was an artistic approach. Maybe in the style of Jackson Pollock, the paint-thrower artist. I love abstract art, but I had a hard time understanding the Bishop family's style of tree decorating. I'd apparently absorbed the Stone morality of the art.

But I gave in, hung a few neat icicles and let Mel have his way with the rest for the sake of peace.

In 1963, another adjustment was required. We had arrived in the US on December 13th, Scott's first birthday. Christy was 6, and Littlejohn was 4. Mom was going to stay with us a while longer in Washington too. Snow covered the ground, and we weren't dressed for it.

Flags hung at half mast, and black draperies framed store-front windows all over Washington. A sad tribute and reminder of our young president, assassinated just 3 weeks before.

We rented a shabby motel room in Washington while we house-hunted and prepared to spend

Christmas there.

Daily we checked on our hold baggage, several trunks full of exotic presents and Christmas decorations plus some of our winter clothes. Of course it didn't arrive for Christmas. We put up a tree, but it stood bare, with nothing to put on it or under it.

So Mom and I summoned our creative juices and enlisted Christy and Littlejohn in stringing cranberries and popcorn, and making ornamental bells out of foil-covered paper cups to hang on the tree. Some kind of foil star crowned the top, and it didn't look half bad.

On Christmas Eve, after dark, Mom and I put on our warmest clothes, left Mel with the kids, and slogged through the snow for several blocks in our light, inadequate shoes, to a drugstore, the only store we knew about that was open, where we bought cheap but colorful plastic toys, wrapping paper, and a few other items so we'd each have one present under the tree.

We'd already supplied ourselves with a turkey and other ingredients for a Christmas dinner which Mom and I cooked, and we ate off the old chipped dishes provided by the motel.

Mel always said that that was the best Christmas we'd ever had. It was simple, there were no distractions such as housekeeping, so it was relaxed, festive, cozy, and memorable. And of course no icicles chilled the air between us.

For many years now, Scott, who still lives with me, is the one responsible for putting up the tree. The rest of his siblings have moved out 20 or more years ago, and he is getting tired of that job. He just doesn't like it. So every year we discuss what we're going to do about a tree.

A few years ago he suggested we just get a shrub. That's what we ended up doing for a couple of years. It was an arborvitae or some sort of anemic tall skinny evergreen in a pot that required him only to carry it in the house and set it down.

That took a little more adjustment for my emotional well-being even than watching his dad throwing icicles at the tree. But last year he gave in and we had a real tree. I suppose this year will be time for the potted plant again.

I've learned to make my peace with the shrub. Actually I think it makes us unique. Already it has provided more memorable Christmases—the years of the Christmas Shrubs.

I had 15 Christmases with Mel. We've had 40 without him, and oh, how I would love to see him throwing icicles at a tree again.

And, albeit belatedly— Oh, how much I've learned from the Christmas trees I've known.

ALL'S WELL THAT ENDS WELL

51

On July 4, 2014, I learned what really happened.

My daughter and husband Rick had some congenial friends over for one of their usual feasts on the holiday. We enjoyed the food and were deep into discussion, witticisms, and relating some interesting stories.

Something made me think of an alarming incident that happened to us when Christy was about eight, and we lived in Washington, DC. So I told the story.

Mel and I were driving from Washington, on vacation to Oregon with Christy, Littlejohn, about seven, and Scott, about three.

I was asleep when Mel pulled off at a rest stop in the middle of Kansas and went in. Shortly Christy decided she'd better use the facilities too. I more or less nodded off again.

I'd had mononucleosis, as a senior in college. Severe fatigue is a major symptom, and the fatigue didn't leave me for years, if ever. That's what I hold responsible.

Mel returned to the car, and we took off down the road again, riding along silently for miles, when suddenly Littlejohn screamed, "Where's Christy?" Our hearts stopped.

Oh, no! We left her at the rest stop. Mel said, "It's been at least 45 minutes."

We left the freeway at the next exit, and headed back, racing against time and the speed limit. I was the culprit. Mel didn't know she had gotten out. I knew it, but in my stupor, forgot to check if she was back.

It seemed like an eternity to get back there. We didn't want to think of what could happen to her. She must be scared to death. And the whole freeway looked the same to me. All of Kansas looks the same. So I wasn't sure I could recognize it when we got there.

Mel finally announced, "Okay, there it is,"

"Are you sure?"

"Yes. It's not much further to the next exit."

Just then, a car came racing up behind us, honking the horn repeatedly, and got our attention. Mel pulled over, and they stopped behind us.

They had Christy in the back seat with their kids and maybe a grandmother. They had just picked her up at the rest stop, and she saw us going by barely in time for them to use the next exit and chase us down, a miracle of timing in itself. They told us how they'd seen her standing there alone, looking forlorn, and offered to take her to the police so they could find us. That would have been a wise solution. But it also would have been a courageous act for these particular people.

They had just picked her up and were nearing the next exit when Christy said, "There they are."

What a relief! We thanked them profusely, and got her into the car with us.

But we couldn't thank these wonderful people enough. It seemed important to get out of the line of traffic roaring by, so we returned to our van, and moved out. I didn't even get their name and address so I could write to thank them and stay in touch. They'd given us a gift that could never be matched and that would stay with us for ever after.

We also tried to apologize to Christy. She must have been terrified. We told her how sorry we were. She, in her usual grown-up, calm demeanor, said, "Oh, I knew what had happened. I knew you'd be back," reassuring us. I actually always believed she had waited patiently, not all that upset over being left.

Fast forward forty-nine years. I told—well, confessed—this story at our 4th of July gathering. Christy chimed in. "Yes, it seemed like a lot longer. I was standing out there by the road, crying, and people came and went, some of them had picnics, packed up and left. Nobody said a word to me or seemed to notice me. Group after group. And me standing there by myself, crying."

That was heartbreaking to hear for the first time. I want to hug that little girl.

At the point in our trip when we lost her, we had just passed by Lawrence, Kansas, where her grandfather, Mel's dad, had lived for a number of years, from the age of five, probably until adulthood, with a little brother in an orphanage. After their parents had separated, their mother apparently thought she couldn't take care of them so dropped them off. Christy told us she was thinking about what it was like in there because we had stopped and toured the building, which she believes was by then a reform school. She told us she thought, "I'll go back and live in the orphanage," not a happy thought. But she knew we'd be back home in Washington, in about three weeks, after the vacation was over, so she could call us then, and let us know where she was. She thought we'd just go on and finish our trip as planned without her?

(I have a different memory of passing through Lawrence. I remember talking about the orphanage and wishing we could see it, wondering what it was like and just where it was. I'm certain we didn't see it. Somebody's memory is failing them. I think she must have just fantasized that to solve her current problem. She thinks I'm lapsing. That's how memories work sometimes.)

At last, after at least an hour and a half of a despondent wait, while people came and went, a nice family came up to her, asked what was wrong, and offered to help. They stood out to her particularly because, after all these people, who didn't lift a finger "even to point at me," she said, this nice family who stopped to help, were African American. And they were the only African-American people she saw that day.

In conservative Midwestern Kansas. It wasn't the Deep South, but close enough. Mel and I doubly appreciated the kindness of these people just because they were black. Not that it should have been an issue, but they were definitely in the minority in that part of the country, and they were the ones who chose to help, even a possibly rotten white family. They had no way of knowing what we'd be like. They did know we were prone to leaving our children on the roadside.

294

This was in 1965, in the middle of the civil rights fight against racism, when so much violence and murders were committed against blacks and civil rights workers. I had done some volunteer work for the Fair Housing campaign, and Christy recognized what courage it had to have taken for this family to have even talked to a young, crying white girl, let alone to have her in their car. They could have been stopped for that. And who knows what might have happened at the police station?

On the fourth when we were discussing this, Christy added that, "In Mom's defense, we were in a van, and I was way in the back where you couldn't easily see if I was missing." Always forgiving. Yes, we were in our VW van, that Mel had written "Oregon or Bust" on the side of, and she'd been asleep in the far rear seat. It also had a horn that sounded something like our old uga uga horns in the Fords. Going through a tunnel, somebody honked that "Shave and a Haircut" rhythm, and Mel finished with the higher-pitched, weak "six bits" part. I'm sure they got a laugh because they repeated it. So it was a fun trip other than leaving our daughter stranded for an hour and a half on the highway.

Here I was, at the party, hearing the true story of her experience for the first time. I wish now, even more that I had made a connection with that family so I could tell them how indebted we are to them. And how much we admire them.

And of course I'm indebted to Christy as well. She protected me for all these years from suffering over the true experience that I'd put her through. The crying and believing that she'd have to go to the "home" to wait for us, missing our vacation in Oregon with the grandparents, and probably wondering if we'd ever truly get back to her. That story tugs at my heart.

It wasn't a bad story to be reminded of on this day of patriotism and togetherness. And to be reminded of the interdependence, goodness, and civil rights of all our citizens.

If only I could find a way to get back to these friends who might well have saved Christy—from any number of bad outcomes that could have happened. At the very least they got her back to us. I wish I could thank them again. Properly.

TODD THE INTENSE

52

Some start slow. Some early. Some aren't interested in anything. Many dabble in everything, sending them in all directions like starbursts that fizzle out as fast as they materialized. Only a rare one tries everything and perfects each venture.

When I was 35 and we lived in Washington, DC, we had our fourth child, Todd. He was born in George Washington University Hospital. All four kids are talented, intelligent, and creative. I say this humbly but proudly. Fortunately they got their brains from their father. From me, there were only occasional times when I did something right by accident. But that's another story.

My word for Todd is intense, and he's of the perfectionist persuasion. Well, I guess they're all perfectionists. (which doesn't mean you're perfect. The extreme is that you can't finish anything because you're trying to be perfect.) But he has perfected more different directions than anybody I've seen.

Todd was precocious from the beginning. Even in the

womb, he was active, nonstop day and night. And as a newborn, we couldn't leave him lying on our double bed as we had the others, because he would kick and move himself until there was a danger of his falling off.

After a couple of weeks, my mother and I were going to do some shopping, and leave him with his dad who didn't seem to be aware of the extent of this. When we cautioned him about it, he pooh-poohed the idea. When we got home he said, "Well, you were right, he fell off the bed." The bed was fairly low fortunately, and the baby was ok.

During those first weeks, Todd would purse his lips and whistle. We noticed this several times, and started saying, "You can whistle!" when he did. After a few times, we started asking him to whistle. He did. On command. I think we usually neglect to recognize that people start thinking from birth. They benefit from conversation more than we realize. Todd awoke me to that.

His crib sat against the wall next to a chest of drawers. After he was able to pull himself to his feet in the crib, but before he could walk, I came in the room to find that he had reached a nearly full little vial of quite expensive Madame Rochas French perfume that Mel had given me, and which I loved, unscrewed the cap, and emptied it onto his bed.

He first walked at about 10 months, so sometime after that, when he wasn't much over a year old, he was wearing nothing but a diaper, after dark, toddling around the living room by himself for a few minutes before bedtime. I came in to find the front door ajar, and he was nowhere to be found until I went outside, down the steps, and across the yard up to the road when I heard whimpering. He had crossed the two-lane road and walked up into the woods in the dark on the other side. I searched him out and picked him up out of the mud. I had no idea he knew how to turn a door knob to open a door.

When Mom was with us and he was still a toddler, she had some medicine she needed to take, so she got Todd to open the child-proof bottle for her.

As time went on he picked up on so many different interests, each one intense. He delved to the depths of everything he touched.

There were so many directions he could have gone. We never guessed then that music would be in his future too. Daddy would have loved his jazz and been so proud.

FRONT PAGE NEWS

53

Every four years I spend several days, doing little except reading about and watching another presidential inauguration. In 2013, I spent the evening before, sitting in front of the TV watching CSPAN through the whole 2009 first inauguration of Barack Obama, a warm up for his second one that took the whole next day.

I love the pomp and circumstance, the masses who think it's worth standing out in the winter cold for many hours to see it in person and to honor the president, the demonstrations of patriotic fervor, the formality of the ceremony. Profound and heartfelt speeches, music and poetry. I love "Hail to the Chief!"

This is the closest thing we have to royal pageantry in this country. Uniformed guards standing stoically, saluting, flags flying, marching bands, floats, gleaming limos. I love a parade!

We have something added though that makes it a well-deserved honorific. Changes in leaders where both sides come together in decorum and mutual respect after hard fought campaigns. This is unique to the United States of America, a display of democracy where everyone works together for good—at least that is the goal— and everybody is created equal. There was a small lapse though, this time, when the president's opponent didn't attend. A first.

Nostalgia for former times crept up on me, not for everything then, but for our life when we lived in the Washington, DC area, our exposure to historic events, and meaningful connection to the beginnings of our country, which school hadn't been able to teach me. Watching the inaugural, I caught glimpses of familiar places, buildings, the historic Old Post Office Building with its clock tower reaching above all other buildings in the capitol and its ornate Romanesque Revival facade, on Pennsylvania Avenue halfway between the Capitol Building and the White House. It reminded me of another inauguration when we lived there.

When we returned from Germany to Washington, DC, the excitement was just as great as moving from Seattle to Germany four years earlier. Both places provided far more experiences than you could possibly take advantage of while carrying on the necessities of daily life. Also in many ways the eastern US is more like Europe than it is like the great Northwest. It was new and thrilling to a couple of provincial Oregonians, (Well, Mel wasn't so provincial; he'd been around a bit more than me, was born in Wichita, Kansas, and learned more in school.) trying to get in on everything and to expose our young children to as much as possible.

We arrived back in the states on Dec 13, 1963, less than a month after the Kennedy assassination, to a city draped in black with radios and televisions still playing somber orchestral and sacred music almost nonstop, in mourning and in honor of the lost young president.

A year later Lyndon Johnson was elected for another term, and we were excited to participate in the inauguration. Mel worked in the Old Post Office Building, in Civilian Personnel for the Department of the Army. The FBI also occupied part of the building.

Several of Mel's coworkers decided to watch the inaugural parade from their offices so we joined them with our kids, and rode the clanking, squeaking old iron elevator up to the seventh floor. It was a perfect spot for viewing the parade from above. We opened the windows and gazed down at the floats, marching bands, and sleek limos with flags flying as they went by. Across the way we saw armed guards stationed on the tops of buildings in all directions. It was a once in a lifetime experience for us.

At some point I think I heard one of the coworkers in the room say something like, "We'd better close the windows." But I couldn't see the point in that. You couldn't see much unless you could lean out the window. Another one said, "Yes, they want us to close the windows." "How did they know that?" I wondered. Shortly Hubert Humphrey, the new vice president rode by in his open limo. I was waving. He must have had some sixth sense because just as he passed, he looked backward and up to the 7th floor, gave me a broad smile and waved! I don't remember seeing the president at this time. He must have been in an enclosed car.

It had been a one of a kind, exciting and fulfilling day when our part of the festivities were over, and we headed home.

The next day it was back to work for Mel and an ordinary day at home and school for me and the kids.

But when Mel got home that evening he had something to show me. It was a newspaper clipping about 3 X 3 inches in size, that had been left on his desk that morning accompanied by a small handwritten note with the drawing of a hand with the pointer, or trigger, finger extended, and which said, ominously, "The" (picture of the hand with the pointing finger) "of guilt points at you!"

The article said, "The secret service had quite a scare yesterday at the Inaugural Parade when some people on the seventh floor of the Old Post Office Building, refused to close the window when ordered before the presidential cars neared the spot." It went on a bit, but I don't remember the details.

I hadn't heard it ordered. I must have been too distracted in the excitement of the moment. OK, I was the culprit. Apparently we, or I, narrowly escaped getting shot by the sharp-shooters across the way. In retrospect I realize what never occurred to me then, that that terrible assassination happened from a window high above another presidential procession just the year before. There could easily have been a trigger-happy guard across the way doing his job.

But we made news. Right in the middle of the front page of the Washington Post. As we used to say, "In the

nation's capital, local news is world news."
  Another first for the Bishops.

HAVE YOU EVER FELT REALLY STUPID?

54

While we were still in the motel room in Washington, DC, waiting for a house, we were shown around the area by a real estate agent. We settled on one in Fairfax County, Virginia, where many government workers live, about 10 miles out of downtown Washington. It would be a 45-minute commute for Mel each way during rush hours.

This was in 1963, and my memory is a little foggy on many of the details 50 years later, but I remember the essence of it.

I must have taken Mel to work, from the motel, not so far from his job, so I could do a few errands including driving to Virginia to license the car and to get my Virginia driver's license.

I located a DMV office which was about a 10 mile drive down Washington Parkway, not a bad drive as it was a pretty straight shot and a few streets off into a little shopping center.

We got moved into our house and Christy into school to finish first grade. Eventually we obtained an old Ford Fairlane so I would have something to drive. The friend we bought it from said, "It's guaranteed 'til it's out of sight." I could go shopping for groceries, and take the kids to the doctor for checkups—all the usual things.

We were there for almost 6 years, so I had to renew the car licenses at least twice, and I went at least one other time to renew my driver's license. I remembered the route to that DMV from my initial trip out there, so I just stuck with it instead of trying to find one nearer by.

So when I had to make a trip to the DMV, I loaded the kids into the car, drove up Norton Road where we lived, a few blocks to a left turn onto Franconia Road, another few blocks and a left onto Telegraph Road by the little IGA store where we shopped, and wended my way through Alexandria and into Washington where I got onto Washington Parkway, and drove down to the little DMV. Then when I was through I had to retrace my route back into Washington to get onto the road back home. A fair jaunt, but not a bad drive, in fact always quite an exhilarating experience driving along the grand Potomac through George Washington's neighborhood.

Much later, after I was pretty familiar with the whole area, and shortly before we were getting ready to move to San Antonio, a friend told me about a cute shop that she was sure I would enjoy. I decided to give it a try.

So—I drove up Norton Road past the other 7 or 8 houses identical to ours in the Burgundy Farms subdivision, turned left on Franconia Road for a few blocks, then jogged left on Telegraph Road at the little IGA store on the corner. But instead of continuing on to the left, this time I took an immediate right onto a little side road that went up the hill. I'd never been on this road before, but my friend told me it would take me to a little shopping center where the store was that she recommended. It was just two or three blocks up the hill. I found it with no problem. There it was right in front of me.

And what a surprise. Next to it stood my favorite DMV.

Not more than 5 minutes in rush hour from our house, counting the time it took to get into the car on one end of the trip, and out at the other. How many approximately one-and-a-half hour, 20-mile round trips through the greater Washington, DC maze had I taken in the last 6 years to get to that place?

You ever felt really stupid?

THE RUSSIAN SPY

55

It came to our attention that there was a spy in the area when we lived on Norton Road. We were in Burgundy Farms, a nice but modest neighborhood. Up a couple of blocks and across Franconia Road was a less modest area with more stately houses, the little IGA store we frequented, the little DMV I went to, the school, and a park. We'd run into a well-known radio commentator who lived over there. It was populated with better endowed folks.

There was some mingling of both neighborhoods at community events and school doings. I led a Brownie troop one year when Christy was in 2nd grade.

I suppose we were listening to the news when we heard about the spy. He had been caught in the parking lot of our little IGA store, providing classified information to the Soviets. They showed his picture. A middle aged man with curly white hair, which surprised me. I had met him when I'd taken the Brownies on a field trip into the park. He lived nearby and was the park caretaker. We stopped and talked with him for a while. Very friendly, he had a little girl the age of Christy that it was clear he doted on. She could have been in the same school or in my Brownie troop. I'm not sure now of the connection. But he was a pleasant man to talk with and welcoming to us in the park. Proud of his little girl.

International spy activity seems like a big thing. And that was so close to home. That particular information exchange happened at our little neighborhood grocery store. And I'd met the spy. Hard to believe. You'd never have guessed he was functioning in that capacity and level. You expect a more sinister character.

The next Life magazine came out with his picture on the cover and the story inside.

Life is interesting in our Nation's Capital.

I never thought that in my lifetime I'd meet a Russian spy.

MEL

56

Of all the things I've done in my life, the smartest one was that I picked the person I did to marry. Of course he was the only one who asked me. But he was also the only real boyfriend I ever had.

The man I married was superior to me, in most ways, and that's the way I wanted it. I've always enjoyed being with people who know more than I do. They're more interesting, and I think help you be a better person. I like being around people I can learn from. But he was also a man of good character, and he wanted the best for people. Wasn't it nice that I also found him attractive—and lovable.

By this I don't mean to say my husband was right about everything. There were two times I can remember that I knew something he didn't. That was so unusual that I still remember them. One was when we were driving through Coos Bay, Oregon. I told him it had once been the largest timber exporter in the world. In fact, more recent research reveals that it was, even then, the largest. So I was under, rather than overestimating it. He sort of scoffed, I suppose thinking that a little backwoods place like that, down in my neighborhood, couldn't be the biggest at anything. But of course, the backwoods is where the timber comes from. I said nothing more. He was used to being right about things.

The other time was when we were living in Germany and took a trip to England. We were driving that time too, through the countryside on a little two-lane road when we came to a sign that I couldn't believe. Kenilworth Castle! And there it was, right around the corner, and just off the road. I was thrilled. "Kenilworth Castle! Right here in front of us. How exciting!" He'd never heard of it.

"Sir Walter Scott wrote a book about it," I told him. He seemed appropriately impressed, though I'm sure surprised, that I knew about that. Of course I'd never read the book and won't. It was a romantic book of historic fiction which nobody has actually enjoyed to my knowledge. But I didn't know that then. I don't know if we stopped and went through. We did visit several castles; many of them look a lot the same, and it was 53 years ago, in 1960.

What I didn't tell, was how I knew about Kenilworth. I preferred to savor for a while, that I knew something he didn't, and to let him live with it for my own amusement until I got ready to confess.

When I was a kid we had a deck of Authors cards and played frequently. Sir Walter Scott was one of the authors and Kenilworth was a book title in the game. I meant to tell him that at some point after I'd milked my superiority for a while. But I just never thought about it again. And there was still time. He also never learned that he was wrong about Coos Bay. Those are just a couple of the little open-ended things left unfinished forever. Among many.

Mel wasn't good at everything. For example, his space

perception was weak. I could always get more into the trunk of the car than he could. But that might be just a gender difference. I've noticed it with other men as well.

His stock answer when I wanted to add a piece of furniture to the house, was, "I don't know where we'd put it." I knew exactly where we could put it, and fit it in with no problem after I'd talked him into it.

He could change a light bulb, but that was about it for fixing things. And he couldn't dance. But neither could I, so that didn't matter.

He was color blind. I don't know that that was much of a handicap to him. Beyond that he couldn't get into the Navy.

I was a little taken aback when on our first date, I bought a red pullover sweater to wear, and didn't think about his inability to see red until I got home when I started questioning what he'd seen. Did that mean that he couldn't see the sweater at all? One of the roommates told him what I'd said, and he had a little fun with that.

Aside from those things, I can't remember any shortcomings.

But he was able to learn; in the army in Korea, he was a radio repairman, of all things, crawling out into front lines under fire, and fixing them in the dark. We just never had a radio to fix after he was home again.

He was highly intelligent. And he was funny. Even in his sleep.

Mel was of average height, 5'9".Once he dreamed about being at some social event where he was standing chatting with a group, and a tall man stepped in front of him and just stood there with his back to Mel. So Mel, without moving, said, "My, that man has a noble head, broad shoulders, tapering down to a narrow waist, and a pompous ass." He woke up laughing and told me the story.

Aside from dreaming funny things, he also had nightmares when he woke me with a blood-curdling scream. I believe that had something to do with a car wreck he had been in. Once when that happened, before I knew it, he was pulling me across the bed diagonally by my foot to save me from something. "I've got you, it's ok, it's ok. I've got you," as I slid off the other end of the bed. Another time, when it had taken quite some time to get the baby to sleep, I woke up to hear him as he stood over her at the bassinet, patting her and messing with her, "It's ok, baby, It's ok. You're ok, baby." Luckily he didn't wake her up again, but not for lack of trying. I finally got him awake and back into his own bed. At least it wasn't some sinister, other personality coming out in his sleep. He was always a caring, considerate person, even trying to take care of us in his nightmares.

Mel was an avid reader, so I didn't always see as much of him as I would have liked because he usually had his nose in a book.

When he joined a speed reading class in Washington, DC, they told him he already read faster than any of their graduates so there wasn't anything they could do for him. I wasn't surprised. He often read a large tome in an evening, his comprehension was total, and his memory seemed to serve him equally well.

He instigated a routine of family trips to the library

313

every other Friday, bringing home 10 books each time and reading them all. The kids each got several, and I got one or two.

Regretfully now, I complained, just a little, that I could hardly dust because every horizontal surface in the house held a stack of books. That was in the days when I still spent time trying to keep the house clean. But give him credit. He did extend himself beyond his forte, and built a full wall of book cases in each of the two houses we owned, for books and a few decorative items. But it didn't take care of the overflow.

He also took a few magazines, which he read, such as The New Yorker, Foreign Affairs, and Playboy.

I still also own his Winston Churchill's 6-volume set, Harry Truman's two volumes, Bruce Catton's 3-volume The Centennial History of the Civil War, Carl Sandburg's 4-volume Abraham Lincoln, three volumes of Schlesinger, Lewis Mumford's The City in History, and the 12-volume History of Western Civilization by Will and Ariel Durant, all of which he read, and which are still waiting to be read by me. It's a matter of time. I'm not a speed reader. Sadly, it won't happen.

I did benefit because he told me some of the high points that they covered, opening up some of the world to me.

Mel always wanted to be a librarian. He would have been a good one. But decided, next best, that we could open a book store on the Oregon Coast when he retired. We fantasized about furnishing it with big leather chairs where people could sit and read by a roaring fire with views of the churning Pacific through the windows. I contributed the idea of turning it into sort of a book and tea. I would provide the cinnamon rolls and scones, as is my wont, to go with hot drinks. He would provide the intellect required for the venture. Of course this was never to be.

Mel graduated at the end of my sophomore year and went into the army for two years. On return, after a year of graduate school, he applied for a job.

It was a new position created by the Department of the Army, called Junior Government Executive. Out of the four western states, Washington, Oregon, California, and Idaho, 33 young people took the written exam, three were selected for the orals, of which Mel was one, and he was selected for the job, working in Civilian Personnel, first at the Port of Embarkation on the Seattle waterfront, then in Fort Lawton in Seattle, for a total of four years before he made a transfer and we relocated to Germany.

Two of his coworkers told me when they first saw him there, they thought Mel was a high school kid who was there to do odd jobs. He always looked young for his age. He was 25 by then. It's a family thing. When we got married, Uncle Guy said to my mother, "Jeanette just married a kid, didn't she?" Mom said, "Well, he's 27." I was 25, but I always thought that eventually people would start thinking I was his mother. His brother also looks young, and our kids do too. Todd was carded on his 37th birthday.

We had similarities in our backgrounds. We were from Baptist families. But they differed in their approach to religion. His were strong Republicans, mine Democrats.

Mel was the proverbial black sheep because he went Democratic. He and his dad had some fairly heated political discussions, but definitely within a loving family relationship. And I clarified some of my own strong leanings with Mel's influence.

Growing up, my family had a handful of books at home. We lived in the country so didn't have free access to the city library, and rarely went there. Mom admired my father for his loving to read. But he read mostly The Reader's Digest and The Oregon Journal.

Mel's mother read mostly Reader's Digest books. Otherwise I don't remember seeing a lot of books in their house either.

Mel wouldn't allow Reader's Digest magazine or their books in our house. Not that anybody wanted them. But it was like a religious belief to him. He thought it was obscene to narrow down to the plot without including the substance of the writing, and to depend on the simplistic answers to everything that you read in their magazine. I'd never given it any thought, but I agree.

He attended Great Books Discussion Groups for some years. Then he led one for five years. It occurred to me that maybe I should go too. We met great friends. Afterwards we lay in bed and talked about the book for what seemed like hours after each meeting. We didn't know if we were so hyped up from the exhilaration we got from the meeting or from the coffee we always had afterwards at one of our houses.

Mel had another great love, jazz music. He listened avidly, understood it, and could almost always identify the musicians when he heard them. I knew nothing about jazz. When I was a music major at the U of O, they didn't believe in it. They called what we loosely call the classics, "legitimate music." That leaves all the rest, including jazz as illegitimate. Now, of course you can major in jazz at many universities, as did two of our sons at the U of O, North Texas State, and USC.

At every opportunity, Mel and I went to jazz concerts when some of the great ones came to town. We saw Billie Holliday, "Lady Day," in Seattle on her last tour. She was weak, and probably under the influence. Sadly a lot of people walked out.

In San Francisco we went to small clubs where we would be within a few feet of these famous musicians. That was new to me, and awesome, to be in such intimate proximity with them. I don't know how Mel became acquainted with the genre, but he had quite a large collection of old 78s and added a collection of modern LPs in our years together.

I still don't pretend to understand jazz. I don't know what they are all thinking as they play. I just know it is highly creative and complex and requires the ability of the musicians to compose and change direction on a dime, or split second, and produce a well-formed structure that holds together as a work of art. The genre is still evolving. Mel loved it and understood it. I grew to love it, but without any intellectual understanding of what is going on.

Mel worked for four years in Seattle, four years in Germany, six years in Washington, DC, and two years at Fort Sam Houston in San Antonio, Texas.

After two years in San Antonio, Mel was asked to return to Washington, DC. He was then "Chief of Personnel" for overseas civilian employees for all the armed services, at 41 and with a long career ahead for him.

So we started getting ready for another move. We felt an appeal in going back to Washington. It felt something like home. We would see old friends again, and could continue visiting the sights. In six years you couldn't hit them all. I was deep-cleaning the house, getting it ready to go on the market.

Mel woke up one night with chest pains. I drove him to the emergency room, they checked him out and said it was a stomach upset. It happened again when he was cleaning the garage a couple of weeks later. The doctor told me his blood pressure was extremely high, and gave him some medications.

He went to work every day. We followed our usual routines. It was clear that he wasn't feeling himself. Once he reminded me not to forget a little life insurance policy he'd had since he was in Korea, and when we drove past Fort Sam Houston cemetery, he said, "You can bury me up there." I didn't want to talk about it.

Mel's parents were on vacation from Oregon, and were coming to see us on their way through. We didn't know exactly what date, but we were excited about seeing them.

One Saturday we decided that Christy could take care of her little brothers for a while so we could go for a couple of errands. She was 13 and always dependable, Littlejohn had just turned 12, Scott was eight, and Todd was three. They were all good kids, and we didn't expect any problems. They were all okay with it too. So Mel and I, for the first time, left the kids alone in the house for a couple of hours. We enjoyed some feeling of freedom, that maybe we could get away for an hour or two now and then in the future.

We were downtown and decided to go on the famous River Walk, just a little ways. We'd never done that. It was so nice, walking with him on that sunny San Antonio day, hand in hand. I wanted to remember this closeness and how wonderful it was to have him, feeling something that I didn't want to accept, but knowing that it could be the last time we might be able to do this. We'd be moving away soon. It was one of few times that I have lived in the moment, savoring that brief time of feeling a special closeness that I can recapture ever after.

We went to a Youth Symphony concert that Christy was in, and for which she played a solo on her cello with me accompanying her. She played beautifully, a beautiful piece. When I came back down and sat by him, I could see his eyes were welled up. I'd never seen that before with him. I touched his leg. He took my hand.

In another week, Mel was having chest pains one evening. It seemed bad. I said, "Let's go." I helped him get a sweater on, and we went to the car. I told Christy to take care of her little brothers while we were gone.

At the hospital, the heart attack occurred. They revived him with a lot of work, several times, and explained that he might survive and be normal, or he could survive and be a vegetable. I opted for survival, no matter what.

I called Christy and the next door neighbors to tell them

what had happened, and that I would be staying at the hospital overnight. Stupidly I assured Christy that everything would be all right. Not to worry.

Early in the morning I didn't see anybody to talk to, but I had to run home and check on the kids, get them off to school, and Todd to our baby sitter, Mrs. Smith. I took time to clean myself up. I wanted to be decent when I heard. I don't know why. I'm the only one who would have cared.

Back at the hospital, I walked part way into Mel's room, didn't see anybody, and was afraid to go all the way in. A couple of nurses came out and told me the doctor would talk to me. They left. I knew.

I heard paging for Dr. Higgins. That was the doctor. Soon somebody asked me to go into a room. I sat on the edge of the chair, trying to get into a position I could tolerate. The doctor and a minister came in. They didn't need to tell me. I first thought, "It can't be. He has four young children. This can't happen." I told them that. I would have thought I would have been in uncontrollable tears. I told them, "I know it looks like I don't care." I was stunned. I stood because I couldn't bear to sit there another minute. The next thing I thought was about all the thoughts he would have had that we'll never know. I walked over to the window and looked out across town. Life seemed to be going on as usual.

He was 41. I was 39. Our lives, and the world, had just changed forever. And I still had to tell the kids.

LUCKY ME

57

The first time I gave any thought to the concept of death, I was 5. As usual I was outside where I did my serious thinking. This time I was sitting in my swing, a few yards out from the camp house where we lived for that year up Coos River.

It was a warm summer day. I don't know what prompted these thoughts. A teenage boy had drowned in the river while we were there, and it was very upsetting to my mother. Maybe that started it.

I looked back at the house and imagined my dad and my mother standing out by the porch, he to the left, she to my right. I thought, "Who do I want to die first?" "Daddy?" "Oh, no." "Mama?" "No, not Mama". I looked back at Daddy, then at Mama a couple more times. I didn't want either of them to die. So I put it out of my mind, giving no more thought to that since I had no control over it and couldn't decide anyway.

When I was nine and living back at our real home at Coquille, my cousin, Darrell, who lived across the road, died from spinal meningitis at 19. He was my cousin

Freddie's big brother, and it was shocking and sad.

I don't know when it started, but I seemed to always know that I would never live to maturity. I didn't worry about it. I wasn't afraid. I just believed it.

My Aunt Nannie, Daddy's sister, the one who gave me a loaf of her homemade bread every time we went to see her, ever since the picnic when I ate most of the loaf and the homemade butter she'd brought, had given me a baby puppy, for my 3rd birthday. He was a pekingese, we named him Toby, and he was my closest friend for his whole life.

Toby was hit by a car and killed on the day of my eighth grade graduation, when I was 13, and he was ten. I was devastated, and sat down on one of our big round river rocks where I did all my daydreaming, and cried.

Not long after that, Aunt Nannie died, in her early 60's. I'd known her best. This was in 1945. Another of Daddy's sisters, Aunt Nettie, died that year as well, which was sad for my father, but I had seen her only once. Another sister, Aunt Kitty, who I'd seen only a couple of times, but felt I knew her well, had died a couple of years before in Idaho.

After a long bedridden illness, three days after I started to high school, my father died, the last one in his family. He was 59; my mother was old I thought, but she was 48. We were glad he had lived to see the end of the war. Roosevelt hadn't been so fortunate. My brother was away in the South Pacific, and didn't get home in time to see Daddy again.

One month later, my grandfather, my mother's father, died after a short illness. They had lived a quarter mile down the road for my whole life. Grandma soon came to live with Mom and me. A year later, Uncle George died. He was the father of 5 of my cousins, close to me.

In 1956, at 25, I was married and starting a new life. We had 4 children in the next 10 years. Mel's family was intact, and we had a wonderfully happy marriage and family. He actually had lost only one person, his grandmother who had lived with them when she died.

In 1959 my grandmother died. She and Grandpa were the only grandparents I'd had as my dad's parents had died many years before my time.

My cousins and I talked about how many funerals we'd attended by the time we were grown, but we never knew what it would be like if you weren't a relative of the deceased. We wouldn't know how to act. We learned that you can survive it.

I have felt lucky my whole life, now treasuring my new family, looking forward to a long and happy life, growing old together and watching our children grow up. I felt so lucky, and said to myself so many times, "How lucky I am!" that we were all healthy and intact. And I often felt I didn't deserve it. So many people don't have the happy whole family that I was enjoying.

Through the intervening years, another uncle and an aunt died while we were away.

In April 20, 1971, Mel went to work, came home tired, and I took him to the hospital in pain that night. He was gone the next morning. The kids were 13, 12, 8, and 3.

I had had 14 years with my father, and I had 14 years with my husband.

The children and I moved back to Oregon to start a new

life.

During the 41 years I've been back, I've lost 5 more first cousins, two aunts and 2 uncles. And I'm not even sure if I'm remembering everybody.

In spite of all the losses, they are all still with us in many ways. They've left their legacies, and we have benefitted.

I've always thought how lucky I am. For a bit, the only thing lucky I could think of was that I was still alive, and I wasn't so sure about that. All you have to do is look around at the trees and flowers, the sky, or your kids. Things haven't been perfect. The hardest part has been seeing my children, grieving at such young ages, and having to grow up without their father. For me, not being able to share the pleasure of them with him, and knowing what he has missed. I regret all that. And we still need him.

But I just have to sit in my swing and put it out of my mind, because I can't do anything about it.

I was 69 when my mother made a visit to our house in 1999, and she stayed on. Eleven months later she died. She was 102, six weeks short of 103. How many people are lucky enough to enjoy having their mothers that long.

She was always there for us. How good that was! She had a hard life, but made the most of everything.

I think about what I have. I think about how bad it is for other people. Two of my cousins lost sons in their early 20's. There are people with dire illnesses and living in poverty, people are victims of natural disasters and horrible tragedies. I've always had a warm bed, and I've never missed a meal.

I know people who never suffered the death of a loved one until they were in middle age. I think my losses have helped me appreciate life more than those people can. There is a contrast that they haven't seen. It is said that for every loss there is a gain.

I've heard some people who had 60-year marriages, say they felt that it was harder on them to lose their spouses just because it had been so long. It is always hard, but I do think people should appreciate what they've had. I hate to fall to envy. But I find that enviable.

I don't feel favored over anybody else nor punished. I know the losses are bad accidents or in some cases the natural part of life. If I thought otherwise, I would be angry with the perpetrator.

I am left with so much. I have more earthly treasures than I ever enjoyed as a child or hoped for. I feel lucky to still be here, loving every flower, every new leaf on a tree or on the ground, and even some of the raindrops. And I feel oh, so grateful for my family and what I have had and still have.

Lucky me!

PAST, PRESENT, FUTURE

58

Snippets of the past, like wood stoves and copper boilers, running boards and bed slats, enrich and fulfill the present, which passes too fast. Fragments and distortions of memories, true but frail, take their place, filling gaps.

The house is gone now. Bare land in its place. Snapshots help.

Babies now grown. Mel missed out. But he did his part, giving them an unsurpassed start. Mel said it. "Eternal life happens through your children." Would he ever be proud if he could see them now. He might even be a little proud of me. (Though I don't know what he'd think if he could see me now.)

I got my Masters, Mel. And I learned to use a computer. Sort of. We even have one on the teak desk. You never saw a computer. Now people wear them on their wrists. The kids grew up, talented, creative, and contributing citizens all, a great legacy for you. They're a lot like you. All of them.

We have four computer nerds in the family, consultants and advisors for me, about computers and everything else. Not to mention their spouses.

And your beloved jazz lives on and evolves. Wish you

could hear two of them, in person and on their records. I try to listen for both of us.

I wish you could know how accomplished they all are.

From sitting on a rock, waving at cars, I have now ridden in some, to places I'd never even imagined. I had an unsurpassed start too, and I've done a lot through the years, but not without help, from my parents, my husband, and my kids, among others.

The best thing is that our kids are all close, friendly and mutually supportive. They keep me going. Everybody loves them. All of them.

And if they don't, they're mistaken.

For the life of me, I never thought it would come to this.

And I wonder what is next. All I know is that I want to see how it all comes out.

Now I'm going to write a book.

And, dear reader, if you've read this far, thank you.

Love,
Jeanette

LAST TIMES
There was a time I had a doll
I held her every day
But now I don't know where she went
Did I put her away?

If I did I don't know when
I suppose I didn't know
I wouldn't bring her out again
I had other places to go.

I used to have a baby girl
But she's a woman now
Somehow I hardly noticed
And I really don't know how.

I used to make her dresses
And hats, and comb her hair
But once I did those for the last time
And I don't know when or where.

My baby boy would often come
And climb up on my lap
He'd cuddle up and smile at me
And take a little nap.

The Bear Came Over the Mountain
Was a song we used to sing.
I can think back about those times
But it's a lonesome thing.

One of my babies used to cry
We had to walk the floor
There seemed to be no reason why
But he doesn't any more.

He was very independent
He'd grab a spoon or cup
Before he knew how to handle them
But he learned, and I gave it up.

I don't know when I fed him last
The only thing I know
Is that I never knew it was the last time
And I still miss it so.

My youngest boy still sat on me
When he had grown to ten
But one day came when he didn't
And he's never done it again.

We used to take walks hand in hand
I knew it wouldn't last
But still I didn't notice
'Til that precious time had past.

When were those last times
That I tucked them into bed
Or got them up and dressed them
Or listened as they read?

And when did they last go and pick
A book for me to read?
I wish I knew what book it was
It's something that I need.

And I want to know just when it was
A toy dropped on the floor
No one noticed as they walked away
To pick it up no more.

You'd think I would have seen it
When they could put on shoes
Without my being there to help
But to me it came as news.

I never knew when the last times were
Just found that those times were done
That I'd missed the end of the special times
Like a cloud had covered the sun

There had to be a last time
That I sang a lullaby
But I didn't know that that was so
That they had learned to fly.

John & Minnie Stone

Me and Toby

Jeanette & Boyd

Grandma

With Cousins Bette & Susan

Bette & Jeanette

Bette thinks this is Flournoy

Valley View 8th Grade Grads, 1944

Coquille Studio
COQUILLE, ORE.

Bess, Verna, Minnie

Bess, Minnie, Verna
with my wig & hat

Minnie & John

With Daddy

Me and Freddie

Boyd

John Stone

Bishop, M., Pvt.

St Peter's Square, Venice

UO Theater, singing "My Mother's Weddin' Day," Brigadoon, 1953

Entertaining the troops, Ft. Lewis, WA

August 25, 1956

Littlejohn, Mel, Christy at Notre Dame

Christy, Germany

Christy,
Littlejohn

Todd, Alexandria, VA

Scott, Todd, Christy, John

Christy, Mel, John

Christy and Scott

Nanna & Poppie in Cannes

Mom in Cannes

Ingenue, Pasadena Playhouse

Mel in Paris

On the Champs-Elysées